MW00572338

Last Days of Theresienstadt

George L. Mosse Series in
Modern European Cultural and Intellectual History

Series Editors

Steven E. Aschheim, Skye Doney, Mary Louise Roberts, and David J. Sorkin

Advisory Board

LAST DAYS OF
THERESIENSTADT

Eva Noack-Mosse

Translated by

Skye Doney and Birutė Ciplijauskaitė

The University of Wisconsin Press

Publication of this book has been made possible, in part, through support from the **George L. Mosse Program** at the University of Wisconsin–Madison.

The University of Wisconsin Press
1930 Monroe Street, 3rd Floor
Madison, Wisconsin 53711-2059
uwpress.wisc.edu

3 Henrietta Street, Covent Garden
London WC2E 8LU, United Kingdom
eurospanbookstore.com

Printed in the United States of America

This book may be available in a digital edition.

Library of Congress Cataloging-in-Publication Data
Names: Noack-Mosse, Eva, 1902–1990, author. | Doney, Skye, translator.
| Ciplijauskaitė, Birutė, translator.
Title: Last days of Theresienstadt / Eva Noack-Mosse;
translated by Skye Doney and Birutė Ciplijauskaitė.
Other titles: George L. Mosse series in modern European cultural and intellectual history.
Description: Madison, Wisconsin: The University of Wisconsin Press, [2018]
| Series: George L. Mosse series in modern European cultural and intellectual history
| Includes bibliographical references.
Identifiers: LCCN 2018013230 | ISBN 9780299319601 (cloth: alk. paper)
Subjects: LCSH: Noack-Mosse, Eva, 1902–1990. | Theresienstadt (Concentration camp)
| Women concentration camp inmates—Czech Republic—Terezín (Ústecký kraj)—
Biography. | Concentration camps—Czech Republic—Terezín (Ústecký kraj)
| World War, 1939–1945—Concentration camps—Czech Republic—Terezín
(Ústecký kraj)—Personal narratives. | Holocaust, Jewish (1939–1945)—Czech
Republic—Terezín (Ústecký kraj)—Personal narratives. | LCGFT: Diaries.
Classification: LCC D805.5.T54 N63 2018 | DDC 940.53/1853716—dc23
LC record available at https://lccn.loc.gov/2018013230

Contents

Illustrations

Foreword   Mark Roseman

The decision to publish this edition of Eva Noack-Mosse's Theresienstadt diary is a timely one. While a number of historians of women's experience in the Holocaust have made use of the German manuscript, currently available online from the Center for Jewish History in New York, an English translation has long been a desideratum.[1] Noack-Mosse's account offers us insights into a group that has still attracted far too little attention among scholars of Nazi Germany and the Holocaust, namely, Jews in what was in Nazi parlance a "privileged mixed marriage." She also writes about a cluster of deportations that we still know very little about—the striking transfers of mixed-marriage Jews from the Reich into Theresienstadt in February 1945. She adds a new voice in describing that strange combination of concentration camp and ghetto that was Theresienstadt, new not least because she experienced such a distinctive phase of its existence. Her chronicle captures not only the last months of the ghetto's life under Nazi rule but also the weeks after liberation. The account introduces us to a robust, courageous personality, one imbued with the virtues of acculturated and educated German Jewish women of the time but complemented by her own insight, humor, and charm, who offers an unforgettable portrait of strength and optimism in a time of enormous challenges. At the same time, Noack-Mosse's diary is not always an easy source to interpret. Part of what makes it so interesting, in fact, is the intriguing question it raises about where to draw the dividing line between memoir and diary, a question of importance for approaching other Holocaust sources too.

Eva Mosse, who was thirty years old when the Nazis came to power, would undoubtedly have made strenuous efforts to leave Germany before the war (and would otherwise have been most unlikely to survive)

had she not married a non-Jew, Moritz Noack, in 1934. The opening
sections of this diary highlight the peculiar situation in which Jews in
mixed marriages found themselves in Nazi Germany. The Nuremberg
Laws of 1935 banned "interracial" marriage, but for various reasons the
regime shrank back from targeting already married couples. As a result,
and particularly after 1938, Jews in mixed marriages would find themselves protected from measures aimed at their fellow religionists (or those
whose descent marked them in Nazi eyes as Jewish). At first sight, this
protection is unexpected. There is nothing in Nazi antisemitic thinking that would lead one to think the regime would treat such couples
leniently; indeed, one might expect the reverse, since the Nazis saw the
greatest threat to Germany as emanating from Jews who had managed to
"insinuate" themselves into Aryan society. But Hitler was also strategic.
He was aware that in order to minimize the risk of reaction from non-
Jews to anti-Jewish measures he had first to increase Jews' isolation. A
steady stream of regulations in the 1930s destroyed the basis for social,
cultural, and increasingly also professional interaction between Jews
and Gentiles. However, existing marriages remained one point of contact between Gentile and Jewish society that the regime hesitated to
target directly (though in 1938, by legalizing divorce on "racial grounds,"
it did make it easier for Aryans to discard their Jewish spouses).

This hesitation became very evident in the weeks after Kristallnacht,
when new regulations allowed Jews to be forcibly removed from their
apartments and concentrated in so-called Jew houses. Jews in mixed
marriages, or at least "privileged mixed marriages," defined as marriages
where the male partner was non-Jewish or where there were children
who counted as mixed race, were explicitly exempt from these regulations. Married to a non-Jewish man, Moritz, Eva Noack-Mosse thus
counted as "privileged." When, as she recounts, antisemitic neighbors
sought to have her and Moritz evicted, her landlords had a clear legal
basis on which to resist the pressure and in fact get rid of the complain-
ants. In the massive expropriation of Jewish assets that took place in
1939, couples with a non-Jewish male partner were not as hard hit as
others, since the husband's assets were not liable to confiscation. When
the Jewish star was introduced in September 1941, the Jewish spouses in

privileged marriages were not forced to wear it—which is why Noack-Mosse was so struck by having to wear one in Theresienstadt. Even Jews in the comparatively small number of mixed marriages not deemed to be "privileged" were generally excluded from deportations—though they were exposed to most other anti-Jewish measures. By September 1944, more than 85 percent of the just over fourteen thousand Jews still living in Germany proper were intermarried.

But as Eva Noack-Mosse makes clear, this was life on a knife edge, or as she put it, life under a cloud. Aryan partners were under persistent pressure to divorce their spouses. The death of the Aryan partner could expose his or her spouse to deportation. The protections were in any case never enshrined in law, and radical Nazi circles continually jostled to end them. Some regional Nazi bosses tried to clear their fiefdoms of Jews in mixed marriages—with, for example, the Frankfurt region setting the pace. Couples in the Noacks' position could never relax; they were always watching the omens. It might well be assumed that the regime would grow more cautious as defeat loomed nearer and as members of the population had to begin worrying about how they might appear to a post-Nazi regime. But the reverse was the case. Particularly after the failed bomb plot against Hitler in July 1944, a radicalization wave took place within Germany, increasing the threat to those in protected categories.

The two immediate threats facing the Noacks in 1944 were forced labor and deportation. In the second half of 1944, and particularly in October, all across Germany non-Jewish partners were dragged out of their current employment to work in the construction battalions of the Organisation Todt. For health reasons, Moritz Noack was sent home almost immediately when he was drafted. In September 1944, in the Rhineland, it was the Jewish partners' turn to be sent to Organisation Todt camps. While this did not affect Eva Noack-Mosse directly, it sent alarm signals throughout Germany, unnerving the remaining Jewish partners. Finally, in February 1945, in a last effort to clear the Reich of Jews, Jews in mixed marriages were to be deported to the ghetto in Theresienstadt. The orders given were made to look as if the deportees were being sent to work within the Reich for the Organisation Todt as their non-Jewish partners had been. As Noack-Mosse notes, she cursed herself for believing this ruse. In the end, she was among only a small fraction of Jews in a mixed marriage who were actually deported. Her account remains one of the most vivid firsthand descriptions of the February transport. It is no surprise therefore that a recent article, one of the few to focus on this final deportation, makes more use of her account than of any other.[2] At the same time, however, it is in reading Noack-Mosse's description of the journey to Theresienstadt that we are also first confronted with an essential ambiguity—is it really a diary? Do we have here a blow-by-blow account of the travelers' perceptions and perspectives as the journey unfolded? Or do we have a vivid memoir, from the vantage point of someone who knows the end point of the story, but with notes from the time to guide her as she captures her recent experience? I return to this question, and why it matters, in a moment.

The core of the account is Noack-Mosse's experience in Theresienstadt from February 1945 until her return home on July 1. Theresienstadt, formerly a military fortress and as of 1941 a ghetto cum concentration camp in the Nazi Czech "protectorate," still figures in popular memory above all as a place where spirit triumphed over extreme adversity. Because it was home to a series of luminaries in Jewish religious, intellectual, and cultural life, some of whom survived, and because the ghetto enjoyed a considerable degree of autonomy, it did indeed prove possible, despite extraordinarily testing conditions, for a great deal of remarkable cultural activity to take place. The ghetto witnessed many splendid musical performances, some new compositions given their first airing there, including the opera *Brundibár* by Hans Krása, which was famously written and performed there. There were innumerable talks (the well-known children's author Else Dormitzer, to take one example, managed to give no less than 273 lectures during the eighteen months she was in the ghetto), poetry competitions, and chamber music concerts. A striking collection of writing, music, theater, and painting from the ghetto has been preserved. Yet remarkable though this all was, it can easily lead one to lose sight of the harsh reality of ghetto life— and Eva Noack-Mosse's account is a most valuable corrective in this respect.

Apart from the fact that she observes life around her with a keen, dry eye and describes what she sees with precision and economy, two things in particular qualify Noack-Mosse as an important observer. The first is her job in the central administration office, which gave her access to the camp records, including the ghetto's statistics. Through her discoveries we learn of the brutal overcrowding at various phases of the ghetto's life and about the horrific shortages many of the arrivals, particularly the many elderly arriving from Germany, suffered from. For these fragile, starving, and weakened individuals, many of whom slept on bare floors for the last months of their life, there was no question of enjoying the ghetto's cultural life. Theirs was simply a futile struggle to survive. As her own knowledge of the ghetto's history grows, so Noack-Mosse helps us put together a picture of the appalling conditions in which so many inhabitants lived. But what we also learn from her is the ghetto's hidden secret—that for the majority of its inhabitants it was simply a transit camp, a holding area before deportation on to Auschwitz and extermination. As the introduction to this edition spells out, 60 percent of the roughly 150,000 sent to the ghetto were sent on to the East (with a further 20 percent or more dying in the ghetto itself). The last round of deportations was particularly shattering, since the relative calm of 1944 led many to hope that the ghetto was being left in peace. But in the month between the end of September 1944 and the end of October over half the remaining inhabitants were dispatched. In late September Theresienstadt was still home to thirty thousand inmates. By late October the population had fallen to not much more than eleven thousand. Only in November were the deportations finally brought to a halt.

When Noack-Mosse arrived in Theresienstadt, therefore, only a small fragment of the original ghetto remained. What she experienced and describes is a community flattened and decimated by continual removals. The October 1944 deportations had focused in particular on those of working age, so that what had been a ghetto with very many elderly people was now even more depleted of lively young people. It is no surprise, then, that Noack-Mosse does not dwell on cultural activities or spiritual uplift. Rather all eyes were on the rapidly evolving military situation, as rumors swirled around about what the Nazis intended to do with the camp. This is the world that she captures so vividly and with such an adept mixture of anecdotes of intimate encounters and synoptic description.

Eva Noack-Mosse kept a diary of events as they happened. But on the cover of the German manuscript of which this is the English translation, we read "written July–August in Oberstdorf-Allgäu." The manuscript that we have in our hands, then, is not the original diary, but an account that makes use of the entries and adds later knowledge. Partly because of this, it also shifts back and forth in tense—though tense alone is not a clear guide to what may have been thought and written when. To make the reader of this edition aware of the process of composition, the editor has helpfully added italics at particular points in the narrative to highlight material that has clearly been added later. There remain, however, many smaller moments where what has been learned later has colored the text, and it is not possible to italicize them all. In the German version that survives, in any case, there are no italics, so the question of what was added when has to be a matter of some conjecture. Though she called her work a "diary," Eva Noack-Mosse was evidently not trying to preserve her day-by-day thoughts and perceptions unvarnished. Rather she was seeking to offer a well-informed account, as objectively as possible, bolstered by as much knowledge as she had been able to gain by summer 1945. Her original diary was clearly a wonderful aide-memoire and allows us to benefit from all the precision and detail she has to offer. What we no longer quite have access to are those original sentiments, fears, hopes, and understandings that later knowledge occludes. We cannot be quite sure, to take one example, whether there were not particular moments of acute fear about what her fate might be that later knowledge that she had indeed survived allowed her to tone down. Conversely, we cannot tell at what point in her trajectory her conjectures about the murder of the deportees turned to certainty. Søren Kierkegaard may be right that life can be understood only backward—but sometimes as historians trying to portray responses and perceptions at the time, we would like to scrape off the paint layer of later understanding and get at the raw sketches underneath. That we cannot quite do here.

In any case, even diaries themselves never come without their own coloration. They are influenced by the writer's sense of her audience, by the conventions that may be attached to writing in a given time and place, and by the writer's own perception of who she is (or would like to be). The self that Noack-Mosse offers us is the very opposite of a fearful victim. She is resourceful, steady, and confident. She may at times be without her comb, her lipstick, or her books, and she may be having to sleep in a rough dorm, but we never feel that her dignity is at risk. She may be at some points a little unsettled at what it is to be "German," faced as she was with Czech suspicions that the German Jews in Theresienstadt might be more German than anything else. But we do not gain the impression that she feels her core identity to be under threat. We cannot know whether the real-life Eva Noack-Mosse quite matched the figure in the diary—and if we were to meet her we might in any case not all agree on what we saw. But we can agree, I think, that the figure that presents herself to us in these pages is lifelike, likeable, and admirable. She brought courage, resource, and humor to bear on the most adverse conditions. She was generous, she shared what she had, but in her account she does not pretend to have forgotten to look after her own needs either. She has a strong sense of what was becoming for a woman—but that included agency and strength, as well as looking one's best, and compassion for others. She also felt part of an intellectual elite, and as such called upon to guide some of her fellow inmates to higher pursuits. She reminds us of that generation of resourceful, educated middle-class Jewish women that Marion Kaplan describes so well in *Between Dignity and Despair*.[3] In the end, it is Noack-Mosse as individual that engages us as much as the tale she has to tell.

Acknowledgments

This book would not have been possible without the support of the George L. Mosse Program in History at the University of Wisconsin–Madison. Director Emeritus John Tortorice first proposed translating and annotating Eva Noack-Mosse's Theresienstadt memoir in the spring of 2015. I scanned Noack-Mosse's typescript of her account and made copies so that Professor Emerita Birutė Ciplijauskaitė could translate the work from German. Professor Ciplijauskaitė was a dear friend and colleague of George L. Mosse and an indefatigable supporter of the Mosse Program. She translated hundreds of pages of Mosse correspondence during her retirement and until her death in 2017. Her extraordinary dedication and energy is greatly missed.

In 2016, I wrote the introduction, retranslated certain passages for clarity, and began annotating the text. Kilian Harrer, then the George L. Mosse Program project assistant, reviewed the translation and further edited for readability. The following text has been a collaborative Mosse Program effort and is richer for the multiple perspectives. The Mosse Program thanks both Professor Ciplijauskaitė and Kilian Harrer for their central roles in completing this book.

Thanks also to the Wiener Library staff, especially archivist Howard Falksohn, for assistance locating Noack-Mosse's postcard and photocopied images. The introduction and annotations benefited from comments by Daniel Hummel, John Suval, John Tortorice, Kevin Walters, and the anonymous reviewers of the manuscript. Their contributions are reflected most notably in the expanded annotations and in the glossary of key individuals Noack-Mosse met during her Theresienstadt ordeal.

Skye Doney

George L. Mosse Program in History
Madison, 2017

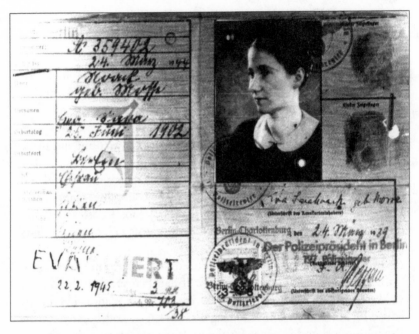

Eva Noack-Mosse commented on her passport: "My identity card with the 'J' printed on the first and second pages. As it turns out, this was an invention of the Swiss government. So they say, anyway." Note the stamp, "evacuated on 22 February 1945, charge 3 RM. Geb.-Buch Nr. 703/38." ("Also miscellaneous personal documents including Jewish identity card," p. 1, Wiener Library Document 504d/1)

Introduction Skye Doney

In the following diary, Eva Noack-Mosse narrates her experiences as a Jewish woman in the final months of the Third Reich. In 1945, she was deported to Theresienstadt, a concentration camp in the modern-day Czech Republic. After arriving in the camp, Noack-Mosse, a journalist by trade, focused on documenting the crimes committed against civilians. She gathered evidence, including statistical information that would prove Nazi crimes against humanity. She looked beyond her own personal tragedies to show the world the extent of Nazi persecution. Eva's experience as a member of a distinguished German Jewish family who was arrested and incarcerated and forced to work as a clerk in a Nazi camp combined with her skills as an observer and journalist enables her to offer an important new view of life and death in Theresienstadt.

Eva Mosse was born in 1902 in Berlin to Max (1873–1936) and Regina Mosse (1878–1938).[1] She was a member of the third generation of a family of highly successful and assimilated German Jews. Her great-uncle Rudolf Mosse (1843–1920) founded a publishing empire that had offices across Europe and distributed newspapers, including the *Berliner Tageblatt*, around the world. Her grandfather Theodor (1842–1916) was an affluent businessman known for his textiles. Eva's extended family designed national legal systems, wrote scholarly works, collected art, commissioned portraits, and were philanthropic leaders in German society.

Her father, Max Mosse, was a physician. Her mother, Regina Laband, was the daughter of the jurist Paul Laband (1838–1918), a professor of law in Strasbourg. Max and Regina had three daughters: Käte (1900–1989), Eva (1902–1990), and Hilde (1904–1998). Käte later married the novelist Leonardo Olschki (1885–1961).[2] Hilde's husband was Alfred Danziger (1895–1979). Both the Olschki and Danziger families moved to California following World War II. Like her aunt and fellow Theresienstadt inmate Martha Mosse, Eva remained in Germany after the war.[3] She died in 1990.

Eva's memoir begins with her marriage to Moritz Eduard Noack (1896–1980) in 1934, one year before the National Socialist regime forbade so-called mixed marriages between Aryans and Jews.[4] The Nazi government classified Eva as racially Jewish because both of her parents were Jewish. As a mixed "Aryan-Jewish" couple, the Noacks existed in a liminal space within the Third Reich. Not wanting to cause civil unrest by forcibly separating couples at the beginning of the war, the Gestapo initially left marriages like the Noacks' alone. At the time they were wed, Eva and Moritz were one of roughly 35,000 "mixed marriages" in the Reich. By September 1944 this number had fallen by almost two-thirds, to 12,487, owing to death, divorce, and emigration.[5] Gershom Scholem's aunt Käthe, for example, was divorced by her "Aryan" husband of twenty years and subsequently sent to Theresienstadt where she died.[6] Because Eva and Moritz married before the Nuremberg Laws went into effect the state could not legally dissolve their marriage. Even so, the Noacks faced harassment; their neighbors, for example, attempted to have them evicted from their apartment, and Moritz was asked by a Gestapo policeman why he had to "marry a Jewess." Like other mixed couples, the Noacks faced pressure to divorce and to stop committing *Rassenschande* (racial defilement).[7] Despite this persecution, Eva and Moritz resisted Nazi pressure and tried to live their lives privately.[8]

In November 1944, after the Gestapo ordered Moritz to report for labor duty in Augsburg, Eva decided to begin recording her experiences. Though he was ultimately sent home, the Noacks interpreted the state summons as an ominous sign of things to come. They were right. In February 1945 Eva received her own orders to report to the Gestapo headquarters in Augsburg. As the war drew to a close the Nazi regime moved against previously "privileged" German Jews by ordering their arrest and internment. As a result, Eva was deported to Theresienstadt.

Following a forty-hour journey, Eva arrived in Theresienstadt on 22 February 1945. She was processed in the "sluice," a stone holding area where new arrivals were held before being released into the camp population. She had to register and leave behind her luggage for inspection, during which many of her valuables were confiscated by the Nazis.[9] Eva was assigned to the Central Evidence (*Zentralevidenz*) office because of her proficiency as a typist. She spent countless hours in the Central Evidence office drawing up lists for the SS: lists of individuals deported to the East, lists of inmates arriving in the camp, lists of food parcels received that would not be distributed to the Theresienstadt population. She was shocked by the variety of people who passed through Theresienstadt before being sent "East": "There were Swedes and Argentinians, Peruvians and Turks, US citizens and Rumanians, Greeks and Italians, Lithuanians, English citizens, Russians, and citizens of Honduras." She "leafed through the lists" that documented the deportation of people from Rhodes, Oslo, Crimea, Salonika, Smolensk, Tunisia, Bucharest, Marseille, Algiers, Riga, Copenhagen, Bordeaux, Athens, Lyon, Budapest, and Kiev. She also kept records for herself, including the death dates of her friends and relatives, and incorporated them into her memoir.

Every day was a struggle in Theresienstadt. To survive, Noack-Mosse maintained a staunchly optimistic outlook. She admired the toughness of those who had already been in the camp for years. She set goals for herself in order to cope with her surroundings. After her arrival, she resolved not to let impatience win out for one hundred days. She had to make it to July, the month she and her husband, Moritz, guessed the war would end. The tension she experienced between feelings of horror and gratitude for acts of kindness toward her permeates her account. She is grateful when her fellow inmates do not comment on her bursting into tears during her first days in the camp. She is deeply moved when her coworkers pool their resources so that she can bathe.

Noack-Mosse's analysis of her lists confirms what historians have subsequently learned about life and death in Theresienstadt. She is drawn to numbers as inviolable evidence of the crimes she witnessed. Through numbers she organizes her memories and ensures that there is evidence to punish those responsible for the deportations and executions. At least thirty-five thousand people died in the camp proper, and another ninety thousand were sent to death camps in Eastern Europe, where fewer than three thousand of them survived.[10] At its height, Theresienstadt housed sixty-two thousand inmates. Overcrowding and poor sanitary conditions, including a lack of chlorine to disinfect, led to a series of epidemics from 1942 to 1943. At the worst point, two hundred to three hundred people died each day during the typhus outbreak in the spring of 1943.[11] Reflecting on the conditions of the camp before her arrival, Eva notes of inmates fortunate enough to survive the various epidemics rolling through the camp, "and they starved."

Noack-Mosse was interned with many German elites in Theresienstadt, but there was no uniform linguistic, national, or religious identity among the inmates. Eva's grandfather, Paul Laband, had converted to Christianity. Her family's identity was not oriented around their Jewish background. In her account, Eva mentions Christian holidays but not Jewish holidays. Like many German Jews, she is disoriented by the fact that the Nazi state has determined her to be first and foremost Jewish. In addition, within Theresienstadt old tensions along national, social, and cultural lines persisted. Philipp Manes, for instance, recalled that the Czech-speaking inmates lumped all "Germans" together, whether guards or inmates.[12] Eva has a similar experience and notes that the term "German" is opaque and sometimes means all German speakers, whether victims of the Nazi regime or the Nazi guards themselves.

The National Socialist government feared bad international press if it was openly violent against internationally renowned Europeans. As a result, the regime used Theresienstadt as a model for international observers to prove that the concentration camp system was humane. In June 1944, before Eva's arrival, the International Red Cross inspected Theresienstadt to review camp conditions. The Nazi authorities increased deportations to death camps and launched a campaign to clean up the camp. In Noack-Mosse's account, the Red Cross returned in April 1945. She describes the surreal quality of the camp, international inspections, money that was worthless, a coffee shop that remained open while inmates succumbed to outbreaks of disease, and meaningless postcards sent home. In addition to figures like Rabbi Leo Baeck and mixed-marriage Jews like Noack-Mosse, the Nazis sent Jewish

World War I veterans to Theresienstadt.[13] The Nazi state intended to jail "prominent" Jews in a central location until the end of the war. At that point the Nazis believed they would be free to move openly against all racial enemies of the Reich.

While in Theresienstadt, Eva researched and tracked the fate of many friends and family members.[14] In her day calendar she kept a list of those closest to her under the heading "death dates." Of the eight people she tracked on her list only one survived: Bianca Israel (b. 1870), who escaped to Switzerland in February 1945.[15] She spent a lot of time with Martha Mosse, her father's cousin.[16] Martha was deported to the camp in June 1943, nineteen months before Eva's arrival.[17] She taught Eva that because some of the inmates were informants for the SS, one should not speak openly on the street. Together Martha and Eva celebrated the end of the war by splurging on Red Cross rice. In addition to Martha, Eva befriended Gertrude (Trude) Zülzer (1873–1968), a painter; Dr. Gertrud (Kanto) Kantorowicz (1876–1945), an art historian; and Elsa Strauss (1875–1945), a friend of her parents from Berlin.[18] They shared food and supported one another emotionally through desperate months. All of these women grew up as members of the economic and social elite before they were labeled as racial enemies of the state.

Noack-Mosse witnesses and records the end of German rule in Theresienstadt. She observes the entrance of the International Red Cross and assists displaced persons in finding out what happened to their family and friends. In addition, she writes about the Russian takeover of the camp and town. Eva offers scholars an epilogue to other camp accounts that end in 1943 or 1944 with the death of their authors, including those by Gonda Redlich, Philipp Manes, and Ilse Weber.[19] Eva was a skilled journalist. The following passage in which she contrasts the coldness of the ruins of Theresienstadt with the liveliness of a pair of swallows near her barracks is just one example of how beautifully she composes her reflections on her internment and difficult situation:

> Thousands of swallows regularly take up residence in the old barracks. The noise produced by people and the constant running in the overcrowded corridors does not disturb the birds. They return every year,

messengers from another world. My pair of swallows seems to be especially animated. They twitter without interruption. Especially just before the light of dawn, around three o'clock, they carry on vivid conversations and wake me from my slumber. I get up and go to the open windows in the corridor. The entire enormous building is full of the twitter of the numerous swallows. The air is filled with their singing and the clapping of their wings. The old ruins live.

Noack-Mosse wrote her diary—tentatively titled in pencil on the first page "Journey into Darkness" ("Fahrt ins Dunkle")—in both the present and the past. She oscillates between tenses—"I receive an order," "My friend was in the same situation as me"—as she guides the reader through the daily life of an inmate in Theresienstadt. At the same time, she thinks back on the things that have happened to her. While reflecting on how important postcards were to her as a tether to her life before the concentration camp, she remarks on what she only came to know later: "Only the first card, which I wrote on 24 February 1945, arrived at my home in Bavaria, six weeks later." In conversations with her friend Kanto they "abandon the present" and journey together to a different world before their deportations, back to the Berlin of Eva's childhood. Still, the camp experience is always at the forefront of her writing, leaking into the past and future. After she returned home from the camp, Noack-Mosse typed up her memoir and used the opportunity to analyze what she had written; she filled in details, consulted historians, and remarked on what she later learned. Her analysis is part of what makes the account so powerful. Noack-Mosse cross-referenced her information with external evidence to prove Nazi crimes. Her later additions and moments of reflection are offset in italics in the text.

Now, after more than seventy years, Eva Noack-Mosse's account of her time in Theresienstadt is finally being published in its entirety. She hoped it would be available to a wide audience much sooner. In 1952 she published a short statistical overview of survival in Theresienstadt in the *Frankfurter Hefte*. Her article, "Diary of a Survivor" ("Tagebuch einer Überlebenden"), drew from the lists she recorded while a prisoner in Theresienstadt.[20] Through the 1950s Noack-Mosse continued to circulate her diary among her friends and family. She sent a copy to her

cousin and historian George L. Mosse (1918–1999) with the hope that
he would translate and publish the work in the United States. In Germany she encountered resistance to the idea of publishing it. In 1954 she
noted, "I know very well that such a report ought to be printed, but you
know these paralyzed and forgetful ducks here in Germany. Who would
want to spend money on publishing a concentration camp report, even
if it contains statistical material?"[21] Still, she continued to hope that one
day the work would be widely available. In 1973 she again wrote to
George L. Mosse about the diary: "The whole matter is too important
for me—even if it is not more than one more voice in the chorus of much
documentation—yet important for posterity."[22] Mosse used the diary
in his lectures and considered it a significant document. In another 1973
letter, Eva wrote to George, "You must certainly remember that I gave
you my diary—many, many years ago, a little after we got reacquainted
in 1951 (?) after your lecture at the Amerikahaus: my diary from Theresienstadt. If my memory is right you found it extremely important as a
source for materials—and also well written; since it is factual, I do not
spread rumors but put down my own experiences and observations."[23]
Toward the end of her life, Noack-Mosse continued to enthusiastically
share her diary with those interested.[24] Two copies of the original German typescript now exist in archives, one with George L. Mosse's papers
at the Leo Baeck Institute in New York and another in London at the
Wiener Library for the Study of the Holocaust and Genocide.[25] The
George L. Mosse Program in History is honored to complete the translation and distribution of Eva Noack-Mosse's memoir she sent Professor
Mosse more than sixty years ago.

Eva Noack-Mosse's journey to Theresienstadt and back home is a
personal journey of confronting and overcoming the camp culture of
fear and uncertainty. Despite the cruelty, death, and disease she witnessed
in 1945 she continued to have faith in human nature: "I am not afraid
any longer. What should I be afraid of? I do not hate people; I have received too much kindness from them." Her refusal to despair was a pro-
test against her arrest and against the crimes of the Third Reich. Through
this ongoing act of resistance, Eva found the strength to document evidence of Nazi atrocities, "in order to help ensure that what has happened
will never happen again."

Last Days of Theresienstadt

MR

(vorläufiger Arbeitstitel
Fahrt ins Dunkle)

Theresienstädter Tagebuch

von
Eva Noack - Mosse

Geschrieben
Juli - August 1945
Oberstdorf - Allgäu
Alle Rechte vorbehalten

Eva Noack-Mosse
D-8000 München 81
Rümelinstr. 12

The title page to Eva Noack-Mosse's "Theresienstadt Diary" ("Theresienstädter Tagebuch"). Written in pencil at the top of the page is Eva's preliminary working title ("vorläufiger Arbeitstitel"), "Journey into Darkness" ("Fahrt ins Dunkle"). The text at the bottom of the page reads: " Written / July–August 1945 / Oberstdorf-Allgäu / All rights reserved / Eva Noack-Mosse / D-8000 München 81 / Rümelinstr. 12." (courtesy of the Leo Baeck Institute in New York, George L. Mosse Collection, AR 25137, box 38, folder 7)

PREFACE

One hundred and ninety thousand persons were forcefully deported by the Nazis to Theresienstadt, a concentration camp for Jews in Czechoslovakia. I am one of the five thousand Germans who survived.

From the very first day to the last, I scrupulously wrote a diary and kept exact records about what I saw. Since I was working in the Central Office in which all lists were kept, I could easily obtain all the documentation and figures that appeared important to me.

The fear of being discovered made me write down everything in Greek letters. After the liberation, of course, I could collect all the material openly.

I have taken care to write the truth, nothing but the truth. About every single fact I did not experience myself I took care to collect reports from several persons. On my own, I undertook "cross-examinations" in order to find out the truth. "Theresienstadt" as a fact is so horrible and unbelievable that one does not need to add anything else.

We cannot wake the dead, our friends, our relatives. Yet we, the survivors, are linked to them in a mysterious way. By reporting about them I pay a certain debt to them. For each one of these [Holocaust] dead did not die once but a thousand times. I have written down how I experienced Theresienstadt in order that their sacrifice should not be in vain. So that there shall never be a second Theresienstadt anywhere in the world.

Oberstdorf/Allgäu
July–August 1945

Contents

The Czechs take over the camp—Arrival of the Russians—The first Americans—Fight against epidemics—Preparations for dissolving the camp—Mr. Graham of the BBC comes to us—Distribution of charitable gifts—Returning home

Nothing was changed in the original manuscript after it was first written. The statistical materials available at that time in Theresienstadt differ somewhat from those published later in scholarly reports. All that appears in parenthesis are later additions.

H. G. Adler, *Theresienstadt, 1941–1945: Das Antlitz einer Zwangsgemeinschaft*, 2nd ed. (Tübingen: J.C. B. Mohr [Paul Siebeck], 1960), appears here as "Adler, *Theresienstadt.*"[1]

In 1934, sometime before the so-called Nuremberg Laws were published, which banned marriage between Aryans and Jews, I got married. Moritz Noack, my husband, is an "Aryan." He comes from a respected old German family that produced many public officials, pastors, and university professors. One of his ancestors, a pastor, gave confirmation lessons to Queen Luise of Prussia [1776–1810] and confirmed her. I am Jewish. My mother Regina, née Laband, was a niece of judge Paul Laband, one of the leading professors of state law of the German Empire, author of *Staatsrecht des Deutschen Reiches*.[2] My father, Max Mosse, was a professor of medicine in Berlin; my grandfather, Theodor Mosse, a merchant, was the owner of one of the finest clothes stores [Gebrüder Mosse] in the capital. He was purveyor to the court (kaiser's family). The name of the firm had such high prestige that an American who had been an apprentice with him around the turn of the century bought the name of the establishment from Theodor Mosse and founded under that name an enterprise in New York that was open until just a few years ago.[3] My great-grandfather [Markus Mosse] was a country doctor in the district of Posen. He had seventeen children, among them a son named Rudolf, a famous German newspaper publisher.[4]

Rudolf Mosse was one of the richest and most charitable persons in Berlin and one of the biggest taxpayers there. He owned a Palais at Potsdamer Platz, which was described in travel books as something worth seeing. After Hitler became *Reichskanzler* the house was immediately expropriated and handed over to the "Academy for German Law," a new creation of the Third Reich.[5] The ample courtyard of the Palais originally had a fountain surrounded by a sculpture with the figures of three dancing girls. For the Nazis, these female statues were opposed to the heroic spirit. They were replaced by stone lions with closed

Rudolf Mosse. (courtesy of the Leo Baeck Institute in New York, ALB-100,
Hilde Mosse album)

paws. The courtyard of the house was located in front of Hitler's Reich chancellery on Voßstraße. Today the remains of the lions have fallen from their plinths onto the ground. Only a wooden cross covered by a steel helmet indicates that this site is the grave of a soldier fallen in the fight for Berlin.

My husband and I lived in Berlin, but in 1941 we moved with the two daughters from his first marriage to a village in Bavaria. We had only one aim: to remain alive during the Third Reich. In the larger cities, the official and unofficial attacks against Jews, mixed marriages, and children of mixed marriages became more and more violent. Unexpected police raids took place. We knew by experience that these actions initiated by Goebbels first raged through the larger cities and then slowly subsided. Apart from that, we were absolutely certain that we could count on our friends in the cities. They would warn us when danger threatened.

It was a punishable crime not to indicate that one was a Jew when reporting to the police. That meant that I was supposed to give my second name of "Sara," which the Nazis forced all Jewish women to add to their real names. We omitted it. After living in peace for about nine months, we started having trouble with other occupants of the house because of our adorable but unfortunately attack-prone terrier. In the meantime, I had more than once received letters from public institutions addressed to "Eva Sara N." Up until then this second name had not been noted. Now, the other renters urged the property owners to throw us out. They acted so indecently that our very upright landlords became angry and decided to give notice to our neighbors, not to us. Since our head of household was "Aryan," there was no law that would have forced the apartment owners to give us notice. Our "neighbors" were the lawyer Dr. [Otto] Stahmer and his family. Later, he defended [Hermann] Göring in the war criminal process at Nuremberg.[6]

Ever since the Nuremberg Laws had been promulgated, all mixed marriage couples more or less openly feared having their marriages forcefully dissolved. There were constantly new rumors, repeated again and again: the law regarding forceful separation of mixed marriage couples is already signed and lies waiting in Göring's drawer. My husband and I seldom spoke about it—we could not change anything. It was a dark cloud hanging over us for many years. After the landing of the Allies in North Africa we knew it was a race to the end of the war, and each day that we could still spend together was a day gained. After the Allies disembarked in Normandy it was clear: the end was approaching.

In the autumn of 1944 the first news about actions targeting mixed marriages arrived from the Rhineland. Married couples were forcefully separated and deported. No one heard anything more from them; no one knew where they had ended up.

In November 1944, the so-called Aktion OT commenced: the drafting of forced labor in the camps built by Organization Todt.[7] All Christian husbands of Jewish women, and all mixed children (who some time ago Hitler had already designated as "not worthy of military service" and excluded from the Wehrmacht) were assigned to forced labor. We trembled at the receipt of every letter. We waited. Our friend and neighbor, a so-called mixed person [*Mischling*], was a bandmaster by profession but had already been doing forced labor in an armory for years. He received a new summons from the Gestapo in November. The text was as follows, word by word:

> You are summoned herewith to report for urgent work service at Organization Todt on 24 November 1944 by at the latest 10 o'clock at the Geheime Staatspolizei-Staatspolizeistelle-Augsburg, Prinzregenten-str. 11 (courtyard).
>
> You should bring along: provisions, food for three days, strong clothes for work, sturdy shoes, one or two woolen blankets, as well as some tools, such as a saw, an ax, a shovel, a spade, or a chopping ax.
>
> This order hereby cancels any contract with your employer. You must submit this order to your present employer. No objections will be countenanced. Whatever is due you from your present employer must be paid by him. Your present employer has to make the following annotation in your records: "On . . . obliged by state police to accept special assignment." He has to report you to medical insurance as "on leave."

Noncompliance with respect to this order will have the heaviest consequences. It is your duty to unconditionally observe the indicated dates.

Our friend was engaged to a Dutch woman, one of those blonde, tough, blue-eyed women who do not encounter any difficulties. Because of the Nuremberg Laws they could not get married. When her fiancé was put behind barbed wire in a Thuringian concentration camp of the OT, she visited him regularly. She climbed over the barbed wire at night to see him and his fellow inmates. She worked unceasingly for him and his sixteen roommates, washing and mending. Every time she visited she made special things—soups and purées—for her dyspeptic fiancé, who spent almost the entirety of his five months confined to bed and unable to work until his liberation in April 1945. In those camps, people were subject to the very heavy physical work of building barracks, and in that particular camp they had to construct a cinema for a group of aircraft officers, since no other work could be invented. It was envisioned that the inmates of that camp would be transferred within a few months to the infamous concentration camp Ohrdruf in Thuringia, where they would be exterminated.[8] Later, records about the death, also known as "departure," of these individuals were discovered in municipal lists.

The camp, surrounded by barbed wire, could not be left by inmates unless they were accompanied by a policeman. Our friend would have liked to see a doctor but would have been required to have a policeman go with him to supervise. Policemen were, however, scarce. So he never had a chance to see a doctor. He stayed in bed in the camp in Thuringia awaiting the end of the Third Reich. And he was successful.

Today he is a bandmaster in a south German city and a happy father.

My husband and I were waiting for a similar letter from the Gestapo to arrive at our house. Perhaps we were still registered in Berlin; maybe the letter had been sent to our apartment there, which had been bombed in the meantime. Perhaps our present address had been lost in Berlin in the chaos caused by constant bombings. Every day was a victory. The armies of the Allies were approaching. We knew that this would be the last winter under the Nazis. Then on 25 January 1945 the registered blue letter from the Augsburg Gestapo arrived at our house. The fiancée of our friend, who had by then acquired great expertise in matters of prison camps, informed us that people like my husband, who had been omitted from the "people's storm" [*Volkssturm*] and from the army because of complex illnesses, might also be remanded to the OT. But how would one know for sure? We had four days at our disposal. We sewed a sleeping bag. Friends provided for us whatever we did not have ourselves. I taught my husband the art of stuffing socks. When he tried, his hands trembled a little. He always pulled the thread too tightly.

I could not accompany him to Augsburg, where he had to report to the Gestapo. At that point the use of rapid trains was forbidden. We packed our provisions: what we had saved over the months. I went to my "iron rations," took the last piece of bacon, the last butter, the last reserve of sausage. The letter from the Gestapo summoned us to bring along tools like a shovel, etc., for work. Since we had also to bring food for three days of travel, our luggage became quite weighty. And on top of that, the uncertainty: would this mean a separation for a long time—until the liberation by the Allies—or was the Dutch woman right in saying that those who were physically totally incapable would be sentenced to be sent back right away? We packed to provide for a long time. My husband went away, the heavy knapsack pulling down his thin body. The hair around his temples looked even grayer when we said goodbye.

If the Gestapo classified him as unfit, my husband could be back home in twenty-four hours. Phoning or sending a telegram had become logistically impossible; air attacks had eliminated any communication by mail. I waited the entire day. Around midnight I thought I heard steps outside. A second later the doorbell rang. I ran down the stairs in my nightgown; I had the feeling I would lose too much precious time trying to get into a bathrobe. I thought I was experiencing one of the most beautiful moments of my life when I opened the door and my husband stood in front of me again. He was shining. Even his knapsack did not look so terribly heavy any longer or weigh him down to the floor. The Gestapo had sent him home right away after looking at his medical report. The Gestapo official had only asked my husband whether he really had had to marry a Jewess . . .

The long wait and the excitement had left us parched inside and famished. We unpacked the food we had loaded in the sacks and sat in bed eating until three o'clock in the morning. We devoured all that we had packed for days of travel, opened cans of fruit, and celebrated our reunion. My husband declared that what gave him the greatest feeling of happiness was the fact that he had brought home our permanent reserves of food untouched, but he said that only in order to tease me.

This happened on 1 February 1945. Five days later it was I who received the registered blue letter from the Gestapo in Augsburg. The text was the same. I got dizzy when opening the letter, and I had to lie down for a moment. I did not lose consciousness from the fright. Never in my life have I lost consciousness. I knew right away: now, I was lost. I would not return home before the end of the war, after the liberation by the Allies. Goodbye to family life; goodbye to a freshly changed bed, goodbye to everything, really everything.

Only those who had a life-threatening illness were exempt from so-called labor service. The decision lay with the official physician [*Amtsarzt*]. I had just gotten over an inflammation of the liver and gall bladder, and a microscopic analysis of the blood had shown an unidentified infection. Our *Amtsarzt* was a typical Nazi physician: young, cold, soulless, cruel, sadistic. He declared even seriously ill foreign workers as "in good health" in order to make them labor in the armaments industry until their last breath. He twisted the arm of one lady, who was obliged to present herself for war-related work and who had already suffered for many years from a paralyzed arm, during the check-up in such a way that she had to take morphine for many days because of great pain. My husband had visited him once. Since he suffered from an inner glandular swelling, the doctor was only supposed to establish the degree of physical work he was capable of. The checkups themselves were too complicated to be carried out in the office of an *Amtsarzt*. As a result my husband had to go to a university clinic every four months. So, since that doctor could not do anything with my husband, he simply asked him: "Do you have lunatics in your family?" My husband, nephew of the German

poet Otto Erich Hartleben, wanted to answer "Yes, a poet." In order not
to irritate the all-powerful doctor, he did not do it. That same doctor had
asked a seventeen-year-old girl, "Have you already been sterilized . . . ?"
And this after she had suffered a serious nervous shock during the bombing of her house in Cologne and after she lost four fingers from her left
hand in a machine accident during her forced labor duty. The young girl
had hoped to be exempted from the war effort because of this serious
bodily injury. She did not succeed. She was not sterilized, hence healthy,
hence able to work.

I knew that I could not hope for compassion from this doctor. If
he had had just a spark of empathy he could have exempted me with
clear conscience. I did have a source of infection in my body. I asked
him with a weak voice for an exemption once during the examination.
He refused. So I did not repeat my request. He put me down as "capable
of work."

From that day on, the day I realized that my destiny was determined,
I started making little notes regularly in my diary.

12 February 1945

I want to go once more to the Gestapo in Augsburg. I want to know
where we are going to go.

On a friend's recommendation I shall spend the night in Augsburg
at the house of a foreign doctor's wife who was in the same situation as
me but strangely had not yet received the summons from the Gestapo.
In my village I was the only one in a so-called mixed marriage who had
received such a summons. There were four other similar couples, among
them the parents of the poet Carl Zuckmayer and the hat manufacturer
Mayser, *whose daughter [Marga] went on to marry the pilot ["Hannes"]
Karl Trautloft immediately after 9 May 1945.*[9] I was the youngest. Was
this the reason? Would the others be contacted later? Everything was a
question mark. The doctor's wife in Augsburg received me with warmth,
in a very friendly way, with such compassion and readiness to help as if
we had known each other for years. At the beginning of February 1945 I
had received a warning: there was an ongoing campaign against mixed

marriages, and I should disappear for a while. Yet at the same time I received word from Berlin: at the beginning of February a campaign against mixed marriages had started there, but after three days the authorities had stopped it. It had become evident that because of the chaos and confusion caused by the terrible bombings the Gestapo could no longer carry out its intentions.

In Augsburg, Inspector [Hans] Grahammer of the Gestapo answered my questions regarding the type of forced labor that would be imposed on me.[10] He said, word for word: "You know, of course, about the OT camps, in which the Aryan spouses in mixed marriages and *Mischlinge* are working. Now, the Aryan personnel there are being drafted to the army. So you will have to take over the work in the office and in the canteen." The exact destination, about which I asked, was not specified. I believed what he said.

For months afterwards, I was mad at myself for having been so naive. What a fool I had been! My instinct had so completely abandoned me that I still believed what a Gestapo official was telling me in February 1945! At that time, I still did not yet know that every, yes, every single word of the Gestapo was a lie.

After that interview I traveled home, rather exhausted. The trains were brimming with weary soldiers; some of them had been traveling for days. I reached Oberstdorf after a three-hour delay. I had only one desire: to make myself a hot cup of tea and to sit quietly with my husband in the living room telling him how the trip had gone and how everything had been settled. But soon it became clear that neither of these wishes could be fulfilled. Early that morning, three refugees from Silesia had suddenly appeared at our front door. To escape the bombings, they had been traveling blindly through all of Germany for three weeks. Now two people slept in our tiny living room, and a third one in the kitchen. It was impossible to disturb these people who for the first time in three weeks were getting a real night's sleep. Our electric hot plate had been broken for several months. A missing part could no longer be obtained. In the thermos there was a bad-tasting barley soup saved for me. It was lukewarm and did not give much consolation.

13–19 February 1945

Preparations, preparations. The whole village knew I would have to go away. Everyone came and asked whether I had a special wish. We thought carefully over what I should take along. Of course, there was help from our Dutch friend, who often visited her fiancé in that camp in central Germany and had thus acquired "camp experience." I did not know where I would go; I did not know when the war would end. And I would not be able to get home before the end of the war. So I had to take along winter and summer clothes, linen for the bed and some dishes, medicines, and as much food as possible. Thus, I took a little bit of everything: my winter dress, since it was very practical; ski trousers, since I did not know whether I would have to work outside; a skirt with a dark, heavy blouse, and another dark silk one—because even in a camp there would be Sundays. I packed sewing necessities and something to clean the shoes with, some thumbtacks, a rope for hanging lingerie, hooks to bind it on the wall, candles, and a pocket light. I sewed a nugget of gold into a piece of clothing and slipped in several pieces of value, because I had to assume that I would need gold after the unconditional surrender in order to pay for a ride on some truck in the great confusion. The summons by the Gestapo did not give any specifics about whether it was forbidden to take along money or objects of value. To start a trip in winter 1945 in Germany without bringing a lot of money and objects of value would have been a folly. I took along the bed linens that had been prepared for my husband. I packed the knapsack several times, trying out whether I would be able to carry it. I had believed what the Gestapo official had told me: that we would be taken to an OT camp and they all were concentrated in central Germany. So I took along food coupons instead of numerous food provisions to make my luggage lighter. I was hoping to find a way to buy some things with coupons in a nearby village. *How stupid I was, and, alas, how unsuspecting!*

I went to the hairdresser and got a new permanent. It sounds ridiculous: how could one think of such a thing in such a situation? But in any case, it seemed important to me to look at least half decent. That permanent cost me three of the precious few hours I still had at home.

Sitting at the hairdresser's with metal curlers all over my head, I suddenly realized how horrible, how inhumane the whole thing was, and I could not stop tears from running down my cheeks.

The last days were full of such confusion that I never caught my breath. They were watching at the town hall of Oberstdorf to see if I would turn in my food coupons and whether those that were not yet valid had not been removed. In those days I hardly ever went out on the street: I just could not take it any longer, hearing the same words of compassion again and again. Then a tooth that had been causing trouble started to hurt again. A dentist had previously treated the root of this same tooth. The pain increased . . . a sign from above? Would the Gestapo leave me in peace if I became ill? We decided not only not to do anything about it but as much as possible to make it worse so that I would present myself in Augsburg on 20 February, the day of departure set by the Gestapo, with as swollen a cheek as possible. My faithful and reliable dentist, a Russian who had fled Russia in 1918, discussed the pros and cons of this with me. Forty-eight hours before my departure he gave me an injection. As planned, the cheek became terribly swollen.

Everyone in these years who said goodbye to a husband departing for an unpredictable war knows how it feels in the last days: taking care of a great variety of matters; visiting with people who come to visit, who bring something precious, say some endearing words, and yet seem like intruders; attending to many petty details that distracts from what's most important: saying goodbye to the closest persons one has to leave. Our oldest daughter had been working as a forced laborer in the Sudetenland for seven months without a single day off. Without being told which auxiliary war service she would have to join, she was transported across Germany and woke up in November 1944 in Westphalia as a "voluntary antiaircraft assistant." The young girl sat in wet clothes next to a floodlight surrounded by mud with a steel helmet on her head. She wrote solitary, short, and unhappy letters, like a child suddenly torn from home for unknown reasons. She was far away, for in the winter of 1944–45, a letter from Bavaria to Westphalia generally took some four weeks to arrive. As a result, the whole burden of looking after the house fell upon the shoulders of our seventeen-year-old daughter, who would have to attend school and now take care of the house at the same time. She had to try to replace me. We had many good friends, and I knew I could trust them. They would do what they could to make life easier for my husband.

20 February 1945

The trip to Augsburg. The swollen cheek and the bad tooth were of no help. The Gestapo official said curtly that I would arrive at my destination after a twenty-four-hour trip and after I arrived, I could see a dentist right away. One last time, I called my husband from Augsburg in order to say goodbye once more. This time, forever . . . "May God protect you" was all he could still say. This time was the last. His voice broke, and he hung up. The swollen cheek had been like a last small straw to which we had been clinging.

I went by streetcar to the assembly point designated by the Gestapo. As I was painfully climbing the steps with my fully stuffed knapsack, sleeping bag, and purse, a man who was similarly burdened addressed me. This was my first fellow sufferer, a man from Augsburg whose wife brought him to the assembly point. I had taken leave of my husband and child at home, since my husband could not use any long-distance train without a special permit. There was no way that he could have obtained special permission to accompany his Jewish wife to the Gestapo, so we did not even try. I was glad to spare my husband such goodbye scenes as I saw in Augsburg. We passed through a barbed-wire fence and assembled in a partially bombed-out building. The Gestapo official called our names. Thirty-two persons had received the summons from the Gestapo. Eight persons had not appeared, despite the threat of the severest persecution. Surely these were single persons who did not have to fear that members of their families would be arrested by the Gestapo if they themselves disappeared. The Gestapo had a habit of arresting other family members in such cases. Among the twenty-four assembled persons, eight were women, which included some mothers who had left their small children at home. Suddenly, two people were informed that they would go to Theresienstadt: a Jewish lawyer with serious war injuries, quite advanced in age, who had difficulty walking even with a

cane, and also an old working-class woman who lamented incessantly as
she walked. Their Christian spouses had died long ago. Apparently,
they had escaped attention during the actions deporting Jews whose
Christian spouses had passed away. Toward the end of 1943 these Jews
had been deported from Germany and from the countries occupied by
the Germans. Two hours before, two Gestapo officials had visited the
old woman. She was told she was to be ready for transport within half
an hour. She was totally unprepared. Since she was not permitted to
leave the apartment, and since a large proportion of her clothes were in
the basement due to the danger of air raids, she could take with her only
the most essential belongings. She had only been able to make a little
bundle and throw a gray woolen quilt over her arm. Her white hair hung
untidily around her head. She had not even had time to send word to
her daughter and say goodbye to her. She had to ask the neighbors to do
it for her. Her son was already in an OT forced labor camp in central
Germany. These two people were now very thoroughly searched. Their
belongings were scrupulously inspected. All the money they had on
them was taken away except for a few marks. We felt great pity for them.
None of us had any idea that we, too, would end up in Theresienstadt,
since our baggage had not been searched. Nor were we asked whether
we carried money or jewelry with us. Before being packed into the busses
waiting for our transport we were allowed to say goodbye to our family
members once more. I assumed this was why we were not told where we
were being taken. Our families should remain in the dark for as long as
possible. All was tears, moans, sobbing. Some months before husbands
had been separated from their Jewish wives and sent to work in concentration camps of the OT, so only friends, neighbors, children had come
to say goodbye. I was glad the parting with my husband was already
behind me.

We were taken by way of the railway station luggage depot. Clearly
the Gestapo had no desire to show us to normal travelers. This might
have raised questions as to what kind of transport this was. As it happened, such questions did come up a few times during the trip, when
we were left standing for hours in several railway stations, next to endless trains filled with refugees and wounded soldiers who were being

taken home to the Reich—a Reich that was getting smaller by the hour. These people always shook their heads in dismay when we explained that we were a transport of Jews who did not know where we were being taken.

We twenty-four persons were assigned an old coach for transport. The SS squad watching us consisted of two men who evidently preferred accompanying transports of Jews to being at the front. We had plenty of room in the coach. At that time, all trains in Germany were so overcrowded that one was barely able to remain standing. In contrast, our fifty-year-old coach with its poor wooden benches hardly seemed uncomfortable, and we were glad to be able to have a seat; the coach was even heated. We were attached to some kind of a train. We did not know where it was heading. We were only surprised that the two older persons destined for Theresienstadt were in the same coach as us. We deduced from this that we, too, would go in the direction of Czechoslovakia—otherwise they would not have stayed with us.[11]

I looked at my companions more closely. There was Ilse, a young woman whose husband was a lawyer. He had to give up his work because of his Jewish wife and was now carrying beams in a camp so that the antiaircraft lieutenants could have a cinema. She was the only woman with whom I could talk about politics and discuss the present situation of the war, since she, like me, had listened to foreign broadcasts regularly and had an accurate sense of the war situation. Her mother had been deported to Auschwitz two years earlier. She had heard no news from her since then.[12]

There was also Anna, an old working woman, with her blonde daughter Trude. Each of their knapsacks weighed fifty pounds. They had loaded them with whatever food there had been in their apartment. Trude, the daughter, had a fiancé who was stationed in Denmark. She had the vague hope that this soldier would free her from the camp.

There was Frieda, an elderly lady with short white hair who looked like a primary school teacher. She came from a small village and had left a seventy-year-old ill husband at home. She was crying because she did not know who would be taking care of her old husband now.

There were also the two inseparable working women Anni and Ilona, a Hungarian born in Thuringia. Their husbands had been together as forced laborers. They were sticking to each other like a burr.

We decided to maintain good camaraderie under all circumstances, and we did. Of course, later we got on each other's nerves as we became stir-crazy. But apart from minor day-to-day squabbles we got along quite well.

21–22 February 1945

We travel, we travel.[13] Now we have found out that we are going northeast. During the night the train waited for six hours in Ingolstadt, a Bavarian city. The following morning the train was attached to some other train. It is snowing lightly. We are going through the Bavarian Forest. We note that we are advancing in the direction of Czechoslovakia. We write the first postcards home. It is totally forbidden, of course, to smuggle mail out of the train. But naturally we do try. One of the men had to get the attention of the SS and start a conversation, while another pressed the bundle of postcards into the hands of a railway employee or some other person who looked trustworthy. All six of the postcards I sent during the trip arrived at home. The men also had permission to fetch water—of course while they were being watched.

Since each of us had photos of our closest relatives, these were exchanged. I admired fat and skinny, bald and bearded husbands, sons in uniform, and babies in lacy dresses. I admired pictures of parents standing next to flower arrangements, which was popular forty years ago, and of babies lying on white furs and kicking the air. And while looking at every photograph I commented on how nice they looked—and thus showed my concern. The world of those we had left was traveling with us. There were few people who, after getting to know each other, did not get out some photos to show. And one had to follow the unwritten codes of courtesy, insisting how nice this or that family member looked, admiring each picture, then listening with patience to the whole story of the person concerned. For what else did we have now but these memories . . .

Our trip lasted forty hours. The two persons whose destination we knew was Theresienstadt were still sitting with us. The SS still did not inform us about our destination, although we kept asking, of course. There was new snow on the ground; everywhere snow accumulated into mounds. Little by little the mountains disappear, the landscape becomes hilly, the farmers' houses poorer, simpler, less well kept, there is less and less snow, and there are bare trees and fewer conifers. We are approaching Czechoslovakia. We pass by Pilsen, gray, dusty, bombed-out sites everywhere, we see the first bilingual German/Czech signs. An air raid on the way. Flanked by the SS, we are taken two by two to some rooms into the basement of a wood products factory. In the meantime, a transport coach from Munich had been attached to our train. First exchange of opinions about our final destination. A lady from Munich thought she had heard the Gestapo request tickets for Theresienstadt at the ticket office. I shuddered. Theresienstadt . . . We knew only that this was the place from which nobody had yet returned.

During the second night we rode, I don't know how many times, around Prague and were, I don't know how many times, attached to different trains. A quarter of an hour on the way, then stopped again for hours. The towers of Prague appeared ghost-like and strange against the somber dark-gray sky. Our limbs were getting stiffer and stiffer from sitting so long on hard benches. The landscape seemed bleaker and bleaker: bald hills, leafless trees, the low gray sky, and poorly maintained rail stations demoralized us more and more. Little by little we all realized that we were coming to the surroundings of Theresienstadt. But we still believed that since we were married to so-called Aryans we would not be put into the ghetto.

The following morning we arrived at a deserted railway station. The two persons destined for Theresienstadt are still sitting next to us. We trip over the rails with our luggage and must form long lines again. The railway station building, with its gray squared stones, makes a depressing impression. There is no sign that might permit us to figure out where we are. While we line up, with our luggage next to us, a railway employee passes by. I ask, with a muffled voice, "Theresienstadt?" He nods cautiously and whispers in the same way "yes." Now I know for sure.

An open truck comes to the front of the railway station. It is going to be packed with parcels. Some strong young men and girls, with the yellow Jew star on their left breast, start loading it with parcels. With the keen eyes of a new arrival I observe the pace at which they are working. It is not fast. The parcels are put in layers with the slow movements of experienced workers. Our luggage was also placed in this open truck.

We march, in well-formed columns, through the village of Bauchowitz, the railway station of Theresienstadt. It rains gently without interruption from the gray sky. The village houses are small, poor, and give me the impression that I am in a particularly bleak part of Poland-Russia. I had previously only seen such a dismal village panorama in a movie.

After the long train trip we found marching on the country road pleasant in spite of the light rain. Our senses were dulled but at the same time more acute. *Still today, I could draw the houses we passed from memory.* Our legs marched by themselves; our bodies followed mechanically. After half an hour I begin to see the spires of a large church surrounded by a sizeable settlement on a hill. Is this Theresienstadt? But we turn in a different direction. Where is Theresienstadt? Invisible! Later we heard that the citadel Theresienstadt had been built on purpose by its architect [Marshal Sébastien Le Prestre de] Vauban two hundred years earlier in such a way that to the last moment, standing in front of the first brick walls, one would not see anything of the town behind it.[14] Before coming to the first fortifications we passed by some very simple houses, and our astonished eyes read "NSDAP Ortsgruppe Theresienstadt." And suddenly we stand in front of the outer fortifications: thick, reddish-brown ramparts from the eighteenth century. An archway leads through the walls. It made me think of the ample fortification walls planted with chestnut trees in Lucca in central Italy. Then suddenly we are standing in front of a city surrounded by a thick, three-meter-high wooden wall. On one side, there was a gate with an elevated turnpike that opened to let us through. We look at each other. Ilse whispers to me: "We shall not come out of here alive." The only words spoken between us at that moment.

That is how we moved into the "city of the Jews."[15] Our homes were far away behind us. Barely forty hours after leaving, we found ourselves in a condition in which home seemed an unattainable paradise. A different world around a different star.

The first Czech policemen in their glaring green uniforms, bright red shoulder straps, and numerous gold stars and cords stand next to the turnpike. They observed our entrance into the camp, the entry of fifty exhausted people advancing like a herd of cattle. The policemen look stern and frightening, in spite of their colorful opera-like uniforms. Later we found out how friendly most of them were, and how well-intentioned. They brought us, that is, to the Czech prisoners, the most important thing, absolutely necessary in a camp—news and newspapers. Their chief was a well-known Nazi, but all the others, like us, secretly hated the Germans and their methods. We proceeded slowly along the street, badly paved, full of sharp stones, and made slippery because of rain. I tried to look through the windows of the poor-looking small houses and kept thinking that my relatives had been living for years in those rooms: Aunt Else [Hirsch], Aunt Toni [Antonie Hirsch], and Aunt Bianca [Israel]—three sisters who had grown up on Tiergarten Street in Berlin, one of the most beautiful streets of the national capital. I would visit them the following day, and they would be happy and scared at the same time when they saw that I was there. What should I tell them? The main thing, naturally: that the war would be over soon, since the day before I had heard on the English radio that the Allies had successfully moved into the Reichswald in the west and that it would not take more than another few months to occupy all of Germany.

We were led to fortified barracks built into the fortress, and the doors opened as we were approaching. Again, not a word was spoken between us. We found ourselves in one of those large buildings with vaulted ceilings, blinding electric light, bare walls covered with chalk. Not a single object in the entire room. On the walls hung meter-high signs. Their message: that all luggage would be examined in the smallest detail; that all money, valuables, jewelry, stamps and gold, precious metals, life insurance policies and other papers of value must be handed in. Not following these instructions would result in heavy punishment.

It would be useless to try to hide anything, since every piece of luggage would have to be left in that room to be inspected, and all possessions would be X-rayed later. We stood there paralyzed, each of us at a loss about what to do with the money and the valuables we had taken along . . . I had already racked my brain on the train about possible good hiding places, when we had slowly realized that we had fallen into a trap. So I buried a small pin in a small piece of butter. *Fourteen days later my luggage that had been searched through and through in every direction was returned to me, and I found the lump of butter and the pin in it. Ilse, the lawyer's young wife, had hidden in butter two beautiful rings inherited from her deported mother. Since the butter was taken from her by SS men who stole from the Jews most of the food they had brought with them, she lost the last farewell gift of her mother. I myself had stuck a tiny diamond in the case of my lipstick, after covering it in rust and gluing it to the lipstick. It turned out to be a good hiding place: the case was returned to me with the lipstick. I stuck my mother's gold watch into an old crumpled paper bag among old crusts of bread. I found both again among my luggage. I put a third valuable piece into a tube of medicine used to stop bleeding and felt especially proud of this hiding spot. I did not know that all medications as well as coffee, tea, alcohol, and cigarettes would be confiscated. So I lost that precious object.* I divided the money I had taken with me into three more or less equal parts and put one part—so that it could be seen—into my pocket book. The second part I stuck into a secret spot within my pocketbook that could not be seen from outside. *This escaped notice, since they did not perform thorough bodily searches at the place where we had to hand our money in.* It was expected that the menacing placards would be efficient enough to frighten people exhausted by nervous tension to the point of practically losing consciousness. The third part of my money I put into the empty sheath of my flashlight, *which was stolen during the examination of my belongings. I could not know that flashlights were one of the most precious objects in Theresienstadt. Thus, they were always stolen during the searches.*

Waiting in those rooms we all had the feeling that our destiny was determined. We waited until we were called, in groups of ten, and were taken to the so-called sluice [*Schleuse*]. The sluice consisted of several "stations." In the first one there was a person sitting at a desk examining the list that arrived with our transport to make sure once more that nobody had gotten lost. Then we proceeded to hand in our valuables. In this room there were German and Czech SS. Two of each. Next to them were working Jews, each with a yellow star on the left side of their breast. In Theresienstadt, every Jew was obliged to wear the star at all times, both outside and in closed rooms, even though everyone in the camp was Jewish—except for the SS, who wore uniforms. *I quickly got so used to wearing the star so that even after liberation I still ran around with my star for several days. It seemed to me it was part of me, and I, part of it.*

At the money-confiscation station we turned in the money we had prepared and received a receipt. *Of course, we never saw the money again.* There was no questioning about or search for hidden money. We then proceeded to the next room for a medical examination. Only Jews worked in that room. From that point on we did not see any SS men for days. By the way, everybody referred to them as "the Germans," which caused quite a bit of confusion for me at the beginning, since I came from Germany. For example, when we were at work, suddenly we would hear "attention, the Germans are coming," which meant we had to pay attention to work and pin the Jewish star on right away in case we had forgotten it. To be on the safe side, long-time inhabitants always carried an extra star with a pin. SS-man [Rudolf] Heindl had once knocked out the teeth of a person who had not pinned on the star. We wanted to avoid that. Since I do not look like a Jew everybody in the office in which I later worked constantly checked, with great care, whether I was wearing the star while the SS was present in the house. For this was the biggest worry: attracting unwanted attention.

Starting with the room in which we had to undergo medical examination, the Jews were alone among themselves. One noticed this right away because the room was filled with incredible humming and buzzing of voices. We, the newcomers, nervous and excited, received our first intelligence about Theresienstadt, whereas the long-established inhabitants wanted to know what was going on in the world and when the war would come to an end. This was the only important question affecting everybody. With touching patience, the doctors and the rest of the staff answered all of our questions. A number of them had been working there for several years already. They must have heard those questions a thousand times already, and a thousand times they had comforted the newcomers simply by being friendly and patient.

The bodily search consisted of two parts: one to look for lice and one of the clothes to find out whether any objects of value were still hidden in them. In my case, while I was being searched for lice, I was placed under a very strong light, which astonished me. I did not yet know the importance of clothes lice in transmitting typhus, nor did I know that many of the new arrivals had spent quite a bit of time in other camps and prisons before the transports were formed. Some of them had spent days in animal-transport trains under very poor conditions. Thus, many were infected with lice.

The next room of the sluice was a large record office. For each new arrival, a very detailed registration card was created. This card not only had personal details but also the names of all family members residing in Theresienstadt so that one could see at a glance what relatives each person had in Theresienstadt and what had happened to them. When somebody died, this "change in family status" was recorded not only on that person's own card but on all cards of relatives on which the name appeared. Thus, an experienced person who held one of these cards in his hand could read from it a complete family history: who had died when and whether somebody had been sent on an eastern transport [Ost-transport]. Later, when I worked in the office, I saw cards with the names of seventeen relatives of whom not a single one was still alive. They had died in the camp or had been sent away "on transport," which almost always meant death in the gas chamber. This unique family card index was to be destroyed by order of the SS in the middle of April 1945. Afterward, only persons who were still alive in Theresienstadt as of 1 January 1945 could appear on the cards. Each card had to be rewritten if it included the name of a person who had been sent away or who had died. The SS allowed the office twenty-four hours to examine all the cards and issue new ones. The office ended up having to partly rewrite seventeen thousand cards in twenty-four hours. The original cards had to be handed over to the SS to be destroyed.

After that we were again lined up, this time without any luggage—I with only my wallet in my hand, since I had—as submissive, obedient, and intimidated as the others—handed over all my luggage, including briefcases, for examination, and had kept neither a handkerchief nor a comb. *What stupidity! I should not have let myself be so frightened. Now I had to sit there for days without a comb or a handkerchief!*

A pretty young woman approached us. She looked like a cross between Eleonora Duse and a wild gypsy.[16] She greeted us with a few words and let us know that she would lead us to the *Entwesung*: an expression typically used in Theresienstadt to indicate disinfection and a bath. It was, however, already midday, and the streets were swarming with people, people who all looked pallid and partially bloated and extremely thin. Almost all wore very, very used coats: the first thing that attracted my attention. All the women had scarves wrapped around their heads. There was no other sound on the streets except for people marching, shouting, and talking. Since there were no vehicles except the private cars of the SS, and there were many things to be transported, all carts were pulled by people. According to the load, there were five, ten, or even more persons pulling the pole of a cart. Since we were not accompanied by the SS guards the questioning started right away again: "What is new? When is the war coming to an end?" We shouted to them briefly, "Soon, surely in a few months," to which they promptly answered with resignation, "Ah yes, we have been hearing this for the last two years."

In the bath, a simple barracks built by the Jews themselves, men and women were separated. The rooms were right next to each other, but our exhaustion was such that nobody cared any more. We took off all our clothes. All the clothes, including shoes, were taken for disinfection. All around us, all naked, a wild confusion of men and women, hairdressers, and bathroom personnel. Some women got ill because of the fright. They were menstruating, and their blood ran down their legs. A new fright: everybody's hair was cut short, allegedly to combat lice. We had just proven that there were no lice, but they cut everybody's hair short anyway. An old working woman who had never had short hair in her life was terrified, but she was helpless.

The personnel consisted mostly of Czechs, and the Czechs, a polite nation, addressed every woman simply as "dear madam." Addressing me with "sit down, dear madam" they meant that I should sit so they could cut my hair shorter. Under these circumstances such use of the address seemed grotesque to me. But at the same time it flattered me to be addressed so politely as a "dear madam" even when I was totally naked. *I found out later that this address was common and that one used it, for example, when addressing an old woman begging on the street: "Don't beg, 'dear madam.'"* Then, very strong liquid soap was pressed into our hands, we were placed under showers and ordered to wash ourselves and our hair. The sharp soap made my eyes water. I had no comb to comb my hair with after the shower. Somebody came to help and produced a comb. It went all the way round. Then we were given old, worn-out but recently washed gowns, and after a while even a large kettle with hot, thick soup appeared. The first warm meal in three days. We had to wait for two hours until our clothes were disinfected, then the beautiful gypsy girl who looked so like [Eleonora] Duse appeared again and led us to our future quarters. "Apartment" would not be an appropriate word for the accommodations.

Like most of the houses, this one was an old two-story building, composed of a ground floor, a second floor, and an attic. These houses reminded me of many two-story houses in Potsdam. In comparison to those, they looked very neglected and dilapidated.

There were sixteen women housed in my room. It was a longish room, with a row of beds built one on top of the other. They were made of old wood in which bugs were nesting. On the wooden frames lay old, partially torn mattresses. My neighbor and I received a torn quilt to share. There were not enough pillows. I did not manage to get one. The walls, like the walls everywhere, had surely not been painted for some fifty years; the paint had peeled off in big chunks. The dirty patches could not be washed away. The many nails in the wall gave evidence of the many things that had hung on it over the course of the years. There was not a single closet where one could hang one's belongings but merely some rough wooden stands leaning on a wall left free above the beds. In one corner stood an old chest of drawers, which contained two tin bowls and wood for a stove. From the ceiling, a gloomy, very weak bulb hung. Stronger bulbs were forbidden. Quite impossible to sew or to read with such light. In front of the beds, there were narrow planks on which one could sit if one preferred not to be lying in bed. The wooden floor was grayish black due to its age, the threshold sinking in a baker's trough. In the corridor, a water faucet and two toilets for the circa one hundred occupants of the house, all female except for the house superior and his male assistants.

That evening we received another warm meal. When we arrived at the receiving station it was announced that a transport of mixed couples had arrived from Bavaria, and they would have to make a place for us. The so-called Living Quarters Administration, which had an exact plan for the remaining free beds, had chosen our quarters for us.

The newly arriving transports were, of course, important news for all prisoners. The news of our arrival had spread like a wildfire. Thus, while we were eating from little borrowed pots, bowls, and glasses, the first people from Augsburg and Munich came to see us. Everybody wanted to get news about their city. Had their relatives perished during the bombings while they were sitting in the ghetto? Had their apartments been destroyed? What had become of their friends and acquaintances? Again, talk, questions, humming and buzzing voices. Again the question "And what about the war?" We told what we knew as well as we could. Little by little the ice was broken. We asked, "And you, how long have you been here?"

I was amazed to see how well informed many of them were about the war situation and all the related events. In many ways we were not able to tell them anything new. And of course, there were no newspapers or radio. Both were strictly forbidden. One had to do with news received by word of mouth, and this news came in an inexplicable way, so to say, flying through the air. Sometimes the Czech police told us what they had heard on the radio; they also passed on some Czech newspapers. Some persons who were working for the SS as cleaners or handymen listened through the walls for whatever they could catch. These were usually just fragments out of which we had to build the story. The SS often listened to English radio transmissions, so actually we were quite well informed about what both German and foreign news reports said. The newly arriving people brought newspapers, which were taken away from them—but the contents quickly became common knowledge. Since most of the news was transmitted by word of mouth, quite a bit was inaccurate. But on 6 June 1944, during the course of the day the news about the invasion of Normandy had made its way to Theresienstadt. Old inmates, who always knew everything, remarked jokingly that they were so well informed that for them the invasion had started a week earlier. Of course, very often false news was widely disseminated. The proverbial molehill often became an equally proverbial mountain. This was understandable considering the way the news spread.

Since we had not gotten our luggage back yet, we went to sleep wearing our day clothes. I rolled up my coat to serve me as a pillow.

23 February 1945

Since we do not yet have Jewish stars we must remain in our quarters. Neighbors bring us very thin coffee, which they went to get for us at the food distribution station. Bread, margarine, and sugar for a week are distributed. The weekly rations in February 1945 consisted of 4 pounds of bread, 50 grams of margarine, 50 grams of sugar. For lunch, a thin soup made of dried vegetables, 200–250 grams peeled potatoes, and one-sixth of a liter of gravy. Once a week, we usually got a small chunk of meat; once, we were given goulash gravy with a few crumbs of meat in it. Already on the first day we remained hungry and began to eat our bread ration at noon. In the evening, we typically got half a liter of barley broth.

The person in charge of the house comes to us—an important person in every house. He is responsible for everything that happens in his house. The house must be clean. It is difficult to keep such an old house clean because we lack proper cleaning materials. The stone steps are so worn out that they have become trough shaped. Whitewash peels off the walls continuously. It is necessary to constantly disinfect the toilets with bleaching powder, since there is no running water in them and many people suffer from diarrhea—thus, there is always the danger of disease.

The house is about a hundred years old, and given the number of stoves must have contained five independent apartments once upon a time. The house superior, a meager, fearful little man, former clothes manufacturer from Bielefeld, has a little office on the ground floor. He also sleeps there. He constantly makes lists, receives messages, distributes notes that come in—and many notes come in. He is held responsible for everything. He also was in charge of picking up and distributing bread, fat, and sugar from the official distribution points. He had already spent three years in Theresienstadt. During this long period, he had lost so much weight that his worn-out suit hung loosely around his body. His dark, melancholy eyes had a friendly expression, even if one could always find fear in them. All of his relatives had been taken to Auschwitz. He had had to endure much in these three years. At times he had to look after two hundred inmates on Bathhouse Lane 2. Now there are a hundred. Few in comparison with earlier days.

The hundred prisoners of the house were distributed in about ten rooms of different sizes. There were still old stoves in five of them. Everywhere the same wooden racks serving as bedframes. In some of the rooms I saw an old, rickety chest of drawers, a few chairs. Everywhere belongings hung on the walls, suitcases were under the beds. Some had already lived like this for four years. The water, one tap only for the entire house, had been installed later. Early in the morning, one after the other—according to when they had to start working—all one hundred women came to that single tap in order to get washed and brush their teeth, if they had toothbrushes. Practically all the women in our house were from mixed marriages; some of them had been there since the winter of 1944. The women from the Rhineland had been deported and separated from their husbands in early autumn 1944. I met one woman who had been separated from her four-month-old baby whom she had been still breast-feeding. When she had heard that she was to be deported she jumped into water in an attempt to kill herself. She was rescued. During the transport she acquired a breast infection because there was no infant to relieve the breasts of the milk. So a woman drank the milk in order to relieve her.

One flight higher was the spacious attic. At the moment nobody lived there. During the most overcrowded months up to a hundred persons had slept there on the bare floor. This was in 1942, when Theresienstadt was overpopulated.

The house in which I lived was in every respect an average building. The street on which it was situated was called Bathhouse Lane. Every street had been given a name after the blocks had been divided crosswise and length-wise. Bathhouse Lane received its name from the bathing facilities located on it. There was a Tower Lane, a Town Hall Lane, a Baker Lane, a Long Street, and a Railway Station Street, thus called because of the railway tracks installed there for transporting Jews into the city.

24 February 1945

I now have a Jewish star and may therefore go safely on the street. I am looking for my relatives. I find nobody, except Martha Mosse, a cousin of my father. The others had died or been taken on so-called eastern transports and workers' transports. No one received any news about any of them. I looked for Aunt Else first. I asked an elderly lady whom I found in a room about her. Aunt Else had been sent to Auschwitz. I started talking to the elderly lady, and three minutes later found out with whom I was talking. This lady, sitting with a motionless face and a partially paralyzed arm, had once been the wife of Heinrich Mann [Maria Kanová]. Mrs. Mann had lived with my aunt for a long stretch of time and was familiar with the chronicle of my family. Uncle Jobst and Tonie, an elderly estate-owning couple from the surroundings of Berlin, had died from exhaustion half a year after their arrival, within two days of each other. Aunt Else's husband [Paul Hirsch] died around the same time as a consequence of dysentery. My cousin Julius [Levin], a doctor, and his wife [Erna] had been sent away on a so-called workers' transport. I heard nothing more about them. I looked for Bianca Israel, a cousin of my father. Her husband, Richard Israel, had been [Paul von] Hindenburg's chauffeur and adjutant during the First World War. He was a racecar driver and one of the first persons in Berlin to own a car.

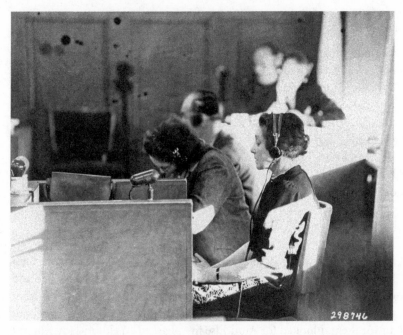

Dr. Martha Mosse testifying against Gottlob Berger, 26 February 1948. (United States Holocaust Memorial Museum, courtesy of National Archives and Records Administration, College Park [Source Record ID: III-SC-298746, Album 5584])

In the photograph of the Battle of Tannenberg reproduced in every schoolbook he is standing behind Hindenburg. What had happened to Aunt Bianca, owner of a famous long pearl necklace made of such wonderful pearls that in comparison the pearls of the English queen did not seem particularly large to me and whose house had been frequented by Lovis Corinth, who as a young man had often painted her grounds?[17] Surprise, surprise! Aunt Bianca had joined the only transport departing for Switzerland on 5 February 1945. I had heard about this strange transport in the middle of February on the Swiss radio, when I was still at home. The radio station had only once announced the brief, laconic news: "A transport of twelve hundred Jews has arrived today in Switzerland from Theresienstadt." The inhabitants of Theresienstadt had believed that this was a new maneuver when it was announced they should register for that transport. Now I could tell them that the transport had really arrived.[18]

I found only Martha. Her beautiful face was swollen, and she hobbled, a consequence of vitamin deficiency. In earlier days she had once been the first woman police superintendent in Prussian Berlin. Now she was the inquiry judge in Theresienstadt. The crimes she had to investigate were little insignificant thefts, break-ins to the basement where the potatoes were being kept (no wonder in a place where people were always hungry), little fights (no wonder when people get all stir-crazy), calumnies, and similar insignificant offenses. Murders or similar real crimes did not occur. I have not heard of a single murder. By order of the SS all house doors had to remain open throughout the night. *The Americans were very impressed by that when they arrived after the liberation and we told them about it.*

Martha gave me—the recently arrived—some important advice: for instance, there were secret police spies, so it was necessary to be very careful in conversations on the street. The SS had forbidden all political conversation—one had to watch out with whom and where one talked politics. The fact that we did it constantly in spite of all restrictions was a matter of course.

25 February 1945

We may write to people at home. We are told that every two months one may send a postcard containing thirty words. Naturally, the correspondence is strictly censored. It is first taken to the so-called post office, which is not a real post office, however, since the cards are merely read there. Then they are passed on to the SS. Since we each have only a single card we write the text first on a piece of paper. *I used to sit for hours in order to produce a card as full of content as possible. I wanted to write that I was "very well" and that I had found a circle of compassionate people. Experienced camp inmates pointed out that the SS tore up all cards with exaggerated statements. It was advisable to avoid mentioning names.* It was forbidden to report about the death or further deportation of relatives. We were also forbidden from requesting food or any useful items. So in the end there was not much more left than to say that one was healthy. The majority did not even use their thirty words. They were too apathetic to be able to reflect on their experiences. The consequence: we all wrote very similar texts. Some claimed that it actually made no sense at all to write. Nothing would arrive anyway. Others just did not want to write anything: they felt so abandoned and cut off from life that they only shrugged their shoulders in despair and lay silent on their beds. One woman was apparently so angry at the fact that she, and not her husband, had been deported that she gave up writing to him. *In the four and a half months that I spent in Theresienstadt I wrote a total of eight postcards home. Friends who did not have anyone left that they knew and those who wanted to do something beneficial for me gave me their priceless postcards as a gift. Only the first card, which I wrote on 24 February 1945, arrived at my home in Bavaria, six weeks later. Nobody knew what happened after the bags of post were taken to the German Kommandatur or whether or not the mail was sent off at all. Having lived in freedom outside Theresienstadt up until then, we all knew only that very little mail from Theresienstadt arrived, which meant that most of the correspondence was being destroyed. I also found out that mail addressed to Theresienstadt practically never reached the hands of those waiting for it so eagerly. For those hermetically separated from the whole world the post represented the only link to family and friends. To try to smuggle mail past the censors and out of the camp was a severe crime. If one got caught one was instantly sentenced to death or handed over to the Gestapo, which meant the same as death. When I now think back about the sins of the Gestapo, the destruction of the mail seems to me one of their worst crimes. Since my days in the ghetto, withholding from inmates the mail addressed to them has remained for me an offense that cannot be forgiven.*

26 February 1945

I receive an order to appear at the work distribution office. I report there. I am too fragile for physical labor and would get too hungry doing it. I decided to spare my energy as much as possible and to strain my body as little as possible. Since I type very well I am put into the so-called Central Evidence office, the main administration office. I have never appeared as ugly as I did when I reported to the office for the first time. I still wore my travel clothes: a multicolored woolen dirndl dress, under it, skiing trousers, and heavy marching boots. The women and girls working with me in the office were mostly Czechs who had already been living in Theresienstadt for four years. All were surprisingly well dressed and had powdered faces and lipstick on. How did they manage to do it? Twenty-five pairs of critical eyes were scrutinizing me when I entered. Since after three days, I was still without my luggage—without a comb, a handkerchief, without powder, soap, or a towel—the only way I had to comb my hair that had been cut in such an ugly manner was to borrow the half of a broken comb that belonged to the old worker from Augsburg. But all were familiar with the woes of a newcomer who had to do without any luggage for days or even weeks. They lent me a towel and two handkerchiefs as well as some money in order to enable me to take a bath.

It did not take long for me to notice what an achievement it represented to appear always decently washed, with tidy clothes, and well combed. Flour was often used as face powder. Newcomers could barter for bits of lipstick. All free time was used to wash and mend. I talked to a lady who reported with pride that in the two years that she had been there she had always had well-polished shoes. I genuinely admired her for that. What inner presence of spirit she had needed for that! This was also the impression I had of my future colleagues there. I admired those who had already lived there for four years: the survivors represented 7 percent. I marveled at their unbroken spirit, their toughness, their morale. For me, newly arrived, every hour, every day represented still a hard task to be mastered with infinite effort. Often I could not prevent myself from suddenly breaking out in tears. None of my colleagues ever made a comment about that. They were well acquainted with the woes of a newcomer. They helped me to get acclimated.

The office was a large room in one of the barracks. Women typed on numerous long tables. The elderly, who did not know how to type, sat at other tables proofreading the typed material and comparing it with the originals. A younger gentleman assigned the work.

When I started as a typist, almost every day transports of mixed marriages arrived. We constantly typed cards and lists of all sorts. I got quite confused at first. What was the purpose of that complex system?

Why did we have to put the name of each arriving person on seventeen different cards and lists? There was a list for the place of departure, another for the birth date; on another, transport numbers, which everyone received, were noted. And the most important: a list indicating nationality. One of the cards was sent to the place distributing bread, another to the house supervisor. I had never seen such a complicated filing system or such great waste of paper and time. I typed slowly, nobody told me to increase my speed. *Later I found out that these numerous and totally useless lists were being created all the time in an attempt to anticipate the insane wishes of the SS. For it happened that the SS would want to have some kind of a list within a few hours—a list that would require several days to complete. Thus, the Jews prudently produced beforehand all imaginable kinds of lists and kept them in stock.*

At my left sat a Dutch woman, widow of a judge in Java. After the death of her husband she had returned to Holland. After the Germans had attacked Holland she had been taken to Camp Westerbork and deported from there to Theresienstadt. The members of her family were taken to other camps. She had not heard from any of them since.

At my right sat a young woman from Vienna, Mrs. R, who became a widow while she was in Theresienstadt. Her husband, a political journalist, had died after much suffering from swine erysipelas in Theresienstadt—an illness that usually affects only animals. Together they had fled back and forth between Prague and Vienna until they were caught. *(After 8 May 1945, the day of the unconditional surrender, I was told by Mrs. R, an Austrian citizen, while we were typing the lists of the dead that "Now we belong to the nation of the winners.")*

In our office there were three other young women who had become widows while there. Their husbands had had no resistance left in their bodies. They had been so weakened by hunger that they had died when attacked by the first illness. The husbands of two other young women had been taken on the so-called workers' transports, and no one had heard from them since.

27 February 1945

Still without luggage. Ilse and I share a single clay bowl for our food. From the Provisions Office, I bring an old knife and two tin spoons.

Ilse has become an X-ray nurse in the hospital. She is desperately unhappy, whereas I am curious and unhappy at the same time. Only on
the first day did I have the feeling that I would never leave Theresienstadt, that I would remain there forever, until the end. But then I noticed
that thousands of people lived only on the hope for liberation and kept
repeating with a confident voice, "Of course we shall be back at home
again." This was comforting; it had to be. When I took leave of my husband we had calmly considered how long my absence might last. It was
February. The Allied troops were fighting in the Reichswald near Goch.
If they could break through the lines, the advancement (we thought of
the invasion of Normandy) might still take some six to eight weeks. By
that time practically all of Germany would be occupied. Then, chaos:
probably another six to eight weeks before there would be a chance for
traveling. So I had told myself I should not get impatient before July. It
was the end of February. A hundred days for a first stay; making it a
hundred days was my preliminary goal. I was going to be patient for a
hundred days.

My roommates, with the exception of Ilse, were simple workers or
belonged to the lower middle class, and they were not as systematic in
their thinking as me. After they noticed that I was always informed
about the situation and the progress of war, they began to ask me,
"When are we going to go home?" I told them, "In summer, but today I
cannot yet tell you exactly when." General wailing: "But we want to be
home by Easter. We can't stand it here any longer." To which I regularly
replied, "Others have already been coping with this for four years." Anna,
the old laborer from Augsburg, wailed, "I could never do that." I said,
"You cannot know this beforehand." Ilse's opinion: "We'll never get
out of here. We'll all be murdered before that. Before the SS moves out,
we'll all be shot or gassed." I thought of the others, who so firmly hoped
to be freed, and said with a firm voice, "We'll all return home." None of
us knew what would happen, nor how. But I *wanted* to hope.

1 March 1945

My life in the office continues. All the women from my room are now
working. Every person under sixty-five had to work. The two women
who were over sixty-five and did not have to go to work took care of

cleaning the room, made the stoves work, and acted as our "room mothers." They took messages and tried to keep our uncomfortable quarters in decent condition. Between the two, the old women fought ceaselessly to maintain the "privilege of the elder" in our barracks of bugs. It was a tough and inexorable fight, fully carried out on both sides, with all the egotism, all the maliciousness, and all the critical shrewdness that old women often mobilize for trifles. The rule was that every newcomer started in the so-called Hundred Group, that is, one would have to do the cleaning and ordering of the room. After a few days one would be sent to do other work. Part of the women worked in the so-called Glimmer: an arms-industry factory that made German weaponry.

Two thousand women worked at the Glimmer for ten hours daily to produce paper-thin laminates out of clear, soft, slate stone. These laminates were used in the airplane industry. Some women were sent to work in the laundry, another was sent to clean the house for invalids, still others to the so-called ceramic workshops, another to a clothing division, where the enormous amounts of clothes the SS had taken away from the Jews on their arrival were being "administered." Women who worked in those rooms were obliged by the SS to maintain a special silence. In those rooms were stacked clothes of incredible value, worth many millions of marks, of a quantity and quality the impoverished country had not seen for many years. Of course, the Jews had taken their most precious, most practical, most durable belongings with them when they were arrested.

The first morning shift at the Glimmer started at 5 a.m., and so one had to get up at 4 a.m. I was the only one in the room who had managed to save a watch. I had worn it under the pullover and simply forgotten about it in the excitement. The woman who had searched me had overlooked it, too. So I was continually asked, "What time is it?" I kept being wakened during the night, since all were afraid to report late to work. This went on, until finally, after thirteen days, Ilse pulled out from her luggage an alarm clock in good working order. Then we all could sleep without worry. The first shift got up at 4 a.m. Lights went on, people got up and prepared breakfast. Around 6:30 a.m. the second shift got up—their work started at 7:30 a.m. I belonged to that group.

Ten days later we are still without our luggage. We sleep on our filthy mattresses. In the meantime, I have acquired a pillow and so can now use my coat as a blanket instead. The mattress is so thin that I wake up several times every night because my bones ache. Since there is only one faucet the morning toilette consists of washing my face with cold water. Then I borrow the half of the broken comb for an instant to smooth out my hair. Somebody even has a small pocket mirror. I had divided up my bread, my sugar, and my margarine very exactly. They were lying on the board over my bed. I wrapped the bread in paper I brought from the office. It was paper for writing, an article much in demand in Theresienstadt. After getting up I prepared my bread: always three thin slices spread with margarine. For each day I had 7 grams of fat and 250 grams of bread available. I sprinkled some of my sugar ration on the margarine. Then Ilse and I went together to the food distribution point. Between the two of us we had just one pot, and we got our weak coffee. Since she had to go to the hospital, which was further away, Ilse drank standing in the courtyard of the Magdeburg barracks, our food distribution point, and left the other half of the coffee for me in the pot. Our office had an old-fashioned iron stove. Every morning two of us cleaned, that is, swept away the dust—there was much dust—and went to bring back a bucket of coal, dusty Czech brown coal, and some wood. We took turns in warming our little pots with coffee and then drank it. Since we would not get anything to eat before 1:30 p.m. I divided up my bread. I ate two slices early in the morning with coffee; the third one I saved until around 10.

A little before 7:30 a.m. we all gathered in a group. Every morning's conversation began with each of us telling how many bedbugs we had killed that night. I was already covered with sores. After a few days I had bedbug bites, flea bites, and a sort of eczema which would come and go over the course of a few hours. My comrades in the office had been prisoners for a long time and thus were experts. After dealing with bedbugs we discussed the war situation. We carefully compared what we heard the night before. We evaluated the rumors, "Bonkes" in the Theresien slang, trying to see what was really true or what might be true. Gerda had hidden a map in her room and explained to us where such and such place was located. Then everyone proceeded to arrange her hair. Every day I admired the way the Czech women managed to create the fanciest hairdos with just a few hairpins. They consoled me, since my own hair was still very short and I could not yet come up with any special style. In a few weeks it would again have grown long enough; then I, too, could have a special hairdo, very modern, with locks high up in the center on my head . . .

Then, work started. Endless long lists had to be continued, cards, lists, cards . . . There was no end to it. The working hours in our office were 7:30 a.m. to 12:30 p.m. In the afternoon we were free until 2:00 p.m. Ilse came to me at noon. She was occupied in the hospital just until noon. She went to get her meal, ate it standing in the yard, and then brought me our shared dish. Then I went to fetch my own meal, warmed it in the office on the little iron stove, ate it in the office, and went home for an hour to try to get some rest. We always started to use the stove by 11 a.m. so that it would be really warm. I felt totally exhausted by the awfully boring and completely senseless work, especially in the first weeks. I had realized after a few days that all this writing was completely useless. The papers of the people that had been deported to Auschwitz and of all the dead had been destroyed a few months earlier. And now we were producing new lists again, which in turn ended up stacked in some closets. I have already explained why we were constantly typing new lists. In the afternoon, we continued to work from 2:00 p.m. to 7:00 p.m., typing and proofreading what we had typed. I can't remember ever having done such dull and meaningless work in my life, work that at the same time so paralyzed and exhausted me. If there was not enough to do at the office, by no means was one allowed to read a book: one was never sure when the SS would come. We finished at 7:00 p.m. I met Ilse at the food distribution point, where we picked up our evening soup. It was either barley, potato, or dried-vegetable soup. We accompanied it with our piece of bread. It was customary at Theresienstadt to toast one's portion of bread. This made for some variety, and it tasted good, and given the watery soup, we craved a bite of something solid and crunchy. When I got home, the questioning started: "Any news? When will the war come to an end? When are we going to get home?" The women sat on the thin planks in front of the beds or lay on the beds and complained about being hungry. The bread they had received was not sufficient.

2 March 1945

Our luggage still has not arrived. Still without a toothbrush. My comrades at the office lend me money so I can go to the baths.

The shower rooms had been installed by Jews. They were open every day; it was possible to take a warm shower daily. This cost three kronen each time. I received this money as a gift. Money did not matter in the camp. Every one of us received a certain amount in paper notes from the bank each month. Of course, it was not real money and was valid only in the camp. With this money we could go to the so-called grocery store once a month and buy some dried vegetables, tea, some spice, and a strong-tasting paste to put on our bread, we could also take a bath, and go to the so-called café.

I went to the shower rooms without a towel or soap. The water was boiling hot and tingly; glorious. Somebody lent me a washcloth. I wrung it out hard several times and used it to dry myself off. Since I continued to be without my luggage I had to put my old dirndl on again. This Bavarian folk dress had already attracted attention in the office. My colleagues asked me if I knew that it was forbidden for Jews to wear German folk costumes. I must have looked very dumb when I heard this. I think my mouth hung open, I was so surprised. But I carefully removed the colorful buttons and ties as a precaution.

3 March 1945

Still without luggage. We have been here for ten days already. For ten days we have been sleeping with our clothes on. Others try to console us. Sometimes the luggage inspection took many days, sometimes many weeks, and earlier, most people never saw their luggage again.

I already know my way around the city. Theresienstadt is a fortress. The name comes from the Austrian empress Maria Theresa. It was conceived as a city of barracks for a garrison of several thousand men and a few thousand inhabitants. It is an artificial structure, drawn on paper and planted in the landscape. The entire city comes to about one square kilometer. In the middle there is a huge square for exercise, which can serve also as a market, with two rows of linden trees. On one side, an uninspiring, sober church surrounded by two four-story buildings; on the other, the town hall in good eighteenth-century dimensions, like many provincial palaces in Italy. Around these representative main buildings are many different houses, some just one floor, others several stories tall with uniform, flat facades.

Throughout the city there are eight relatively large barracks in which thousands of people were accommodated. The private houses, mainly just one floor, all very similar, were mostly built around the same time. With the exception of just a few, all have flat, simple facades. The houses are grouped in four-cornered blocks so that one group always has a common courtyard.

But some single-story and even multistory buildings were built into the courtyards, giving rise to a maze of interconnected yards, corners, and passages in which it is easy to get lost. People from Hamburg were reminded of their narrow alleyways. Countless entrances in the back, dirty corners, little cottages and sheds; countless garbage cans and heaps of rubble. In the courtyards: cesspools, clotheslines, at times a little tree, a minuscule flowerbed.

There are stores on the streets, but you cannot buy anything there. You must have a permit, for which you'll receive only old, already used, and worn-out merchandise. In the shop windows the most beautiful lingerie is displayed, as well as special, distinguished leather products: objects taken away from the Jews on their arrival. The Jews, knowing that they would be deported, had of course taken with them useful things of lasting, good quality. The greater part of them never saw any of their luggage again. Some people did later see some of the things that had been taken away from them displayed in shop windows. But almost none had enough money to purchase them back. These shops were established when the first International Commission was expected to make its inspection. But we'll speak of that at another point.

The city, a little garrison town, was originally established for six to seven thousand inhabitants including soldiers. *When Theresienstadt was converted to a camp for Jews, up to sixty thousand people were concentrated there at times.* When I arrived, there were seventeen thousand occupants. I found Theresienstadt overcrowded as it was, and the mass of people moving around me oppressive.

There was a little old city park, five broad and ten narrow streets. Some streets were paved with cobblestones. It was very difficult to walk on them. Some streets were not paved at all. When it rained, the dusty ground was quickly transformed into a muddy morass.

The city was encircled by walls and fortifications. From the summer of 1944 on prisoners were permitted to walk on the walls. The enchanted view overlooked a hilly, undulating landscape with mountains in the background, some softly rising, some partly volcanic and standing like abruptly formed mole mounds. The view wanders over fields, country roads, tree-lined avenues, and little winding streams. A romantic [Joseph von] Eichendorff and [Adalbert] Stifter [1805–1868] landscape.[19] The eye caresses the soft lines of the mountains that gaze down on the main road, a warning and consolation at the same time. The sky is wide open, reminiscent of Italy with its colorful sunsets, its magnificent formations of clouds, its many shades of blue, from the deepest royal blue to faint purple, from soft yellow to densely toned turquoise. When Martha [Mosse] and I sat on the walls, and our ever newly enchanted eye wandered with delight around the landscape, we felt time and again the perfection of nature and the imperfection of man. The land had been cultivated by the hands of man centuries ago. The hands of man had planted trees along the winding rivers. The hands of man had ploughed the surrounding fields. The hands of man had reaped the crops and would still do so when what is today became the past: a camp of prisoners leading an artificial life and waiting for their annihilation.

We do not know exactly when the plan to transform Theresienstadt into a city for Jews was conceived.[20] *(After the archives were opened, it was found out that the SS had decided on 19 October 1941 to transform Theresienstadt into a ghetto.)*[21] At any rate, the houses in this small, former garrison town were expropriated and their owners forced to leave. *Shortly after the liberation in 1945 a number of them came back and were horrified to see what their houses had become.* In the few newer and more modern houses that had had a bathroom, the bathtubs had been removed so that more people could be accommodated in them.

In the days of overpopulation, it was calculated that the allocation of space should be 1.80 square meters per person. At the end of 1941 the first Czech Jews arrived and found empty houses.[22] For months they slept on bare floors. Even in 1943, a seventy-five-year old uncle of mine [Richard Israel] had to sleep on a cold, bare floor for the last six months of his life. Little by little, rough two-level wooden beds were fabricated. These wood constructions were soon occupied by bedbugs. They have proven impossible to chase from either the bed frames or the old walls. From time to time entire houses were fumigated and gassed because of the bedbugs. But after a little while the bedbugs came back. You'd have to burn the entire city in order to destroy the bedbugs for good.

In summer, a good part of the inhabitants moved to the yards to sleep. The bedbug plague was especially intolerable during the summer. Some people always slept with the lights on. They had somehow got hold of very strong light bulbs and simply left the lights on all night with tightly drawn drapes. Because bedbugs can't stand the light.

In Germany, we all had seen the pictures in the Goebbels newsreels showing the apartments from the so-called Soviet paradise. They looked like residences of the upper bourgeoisie when compared to the living conditions of an inmate in Theresienstadt. In general, prisoners had at their disposal a bed and the space behind it for their belongings. Their clothes hung on the stained walls behind some drapes. People placed pots and pans, bowls, toiletries, and other little necessary objects on a wooden plank above the bed. Under the bed, they kept suitcases with clothes, linen, etc., if they had not been stolen on arrival. Many persons had lived like that for four years. Most of the old houses had no modern equipment whatsoever. It was the Jews who had brought water installations into the houses and built showers. First-class pioneer work.

The stone steps in the stairwells, worn out over the centuries, had the shape of deep troughs, similar to those used by bakers for kneading dough. The hallways had suffered from long use; they were so uneven that when it was dark people slipped and fell. Almost every room had a small round iron stove that could be used to warm up food. Until the end of the war there was not much coal, but it was almost enough, even if of poor quality. But the people who came from Germany, used to cold rooms during the war, were grateful for the little heat they got.

In the big barracks there were many huge rooms with a corresponding mass of people in each of them. It was common to cram more than one hundred people in a room. So they lived, one on top of the other—including people who had earlier each owned their own private homes. They were never alone. During the day they worked in factories or offices; at night, their only "personal" place was the bed. Even in the toilet they were not alone initially. As in soldiers' barracks, the toilets were only long rows of holes.

Only a few inmates lived in slightly more humane quarters. These were the employees who worked in the large offices of the Magdeburger barracks. All of the camp offices were located in these enormous military quarters.

Theoretically, Theresienstadt was an "autonomous administration." The SS invented this fancy-sounding title. Apart from the Central Evidence office, in which I sat typing endless lists and index cards of all colors ten hours per day, there was, in addition, a work pool, a Labor Welfare Office, an office for meal cards, etc. Since there was no money except for a few kronen, countless little receipts had to be written. The kronen represented a kind of pocket money, but the inhabitants had to use those receipts to have new soles put on their shoes, to have their clothes washed, and have small repairs made on their wardrobe. As a consequence of that whole economic system there was constant, meaningless activity in all the offices. There were more offices and desks generating cards than workshops. The workshops could not do much more than patch up the increasingly deteriorating property anyway. So, for instance, there was a large office with the high-sounding name "Construction Office" and another with the pretentious name "Relief" that had the thankless task of making life easier for the poor and elderly. I went to that office on one of my first days when I had not yet received my luggage—which meant no spoon, no fork for eating. At that time, I did not yet know my colleagues in the office well enough to ask them about it. The Relief Office was a shop of trash; from a heap of rusty, bent, damaged spoons, forks, and knives, I picked the best for my needs. The whole shop reeked of poverty. Total poverty, total *Lumpenproletariat*, to which the cultivated Jews were forced back. Far, far away, there was somewhere at home a light-colored case lined with white satin containing my silver knife, fork, and spoon, which had been given to me at my birth by my uncle Salomon Mosse [1837–1903]. With the gift had come a finely engraved business card that I had carefully preserved. Its shine was fading far, far behind me.

And there was the Council of the Elders and the so-called leadership, the man who received orders from the office of the SS and had to carry them out—the most difficult and delicate job in the whole ghetto. From among the numerous directors of that office who had succeeded each other only the last one has survived. All the others were picked up one after the other by the Gestapo. The last mayor was a robust Jew from the East [Benjamin Murmelstein], who had the outer appearance of a boxer or a butcher.[23] Unlike all his predecessors—cultivated idealists and as such incapable of resisting the dirty tricks of the SS—he was a firm, clever Jew. Thanks to his primitive and cunning slyness, he managed to get the better of the SS.

7 March 1945

Our luggage is made available. We go to the discharging place, and everyone is trying to find their belongings. One has to sign a receipt for the luggage one has received. It looks as if everything was being carried out in an honest way. Unfortunately, once more it only appears honest. From each piece of luggage something has been stolen. From some more, from others less. Medicines, tobacco, and alcohol are considered "contraband"—they have all been stolen. Everybody found something missing from the food they had brought along. From me, they stole a two-pound ham that my husband had purchased on the black market for 130 marks, a small bottle of cognac sacrificed by friends, half a pound of coffee, two pairs of new stockings, candles, hairpins, and a new lipstick. But with the tea that had been left, four small precious pieces of soap, two pounds of sugar, and a bag of dried apples, I celebrated a rapturous reunion.

With a little piece of soap I won the heart of one of the women who distributed the meals. She was not always on duty, but when she was I could be assured that for that meal I would be cared for. Every one of us had a friend at that important place. Everyone, proceeding through the long line, looked out for the person who would fill the ladle to the brim, who would reach to the bottom of the thin soup and bring up some thick substance. So I conquered the heart of a big pleasant woman from Mannheim with a small piece of rich, good soap. *My best day with her was one on which she was dishing out the food right when the International Commission was inspecting the camp—on that day, of course, there was a princely meal: vegetable soup and meat balls and potatoes for lunch, and a lentil soup for supper.*[24] *That soup, of which I took three servings, since I was the only person at the food counter, was the most wonderful lentil soup I had tasted in my life until that point. I felt so full after that meal that I could hardly walk. I was entirely satisfied and had the feeling that after such soup I could never be hungry again.*

8 March 1945

I go to the office with a clean blouse, clean skirt, freshly brushed hair, freshly washed face, and freshly perfumed—my husband had given me a small flask of Guerlain perfume, "just in case, and for consolation," as he said. A general "ah" on all sides. Everybody looks at me closely, every piece of my clothes is admired and discussed in detail. It has been years since any of the girls have smelled a drop of perfume. Everyone is sniffing the air around me. A few drops of French perfume magically transform the barren office. Everyone comes quite close to me in order to sniff around. The following day I bring the little flask to the office so that everyone can get a few drops. That was quite fun. Even the oldest women, thin, gray haired, half dead, who had been proofreading countless lists of names for days, months, years—even they did not have such sad, extinguished eyes after putting on a little perfume.

10 March 1945

I type ten hours every day. At times I type senseless lines that revolt me and it is becoming unbearable little by little. So, for instance, I had to type the following list on this day, of which I made a copy:

Theresienstadt, 10 March 1945

Listing of food items, sewing materials, and medicaments received from the Red Cross and kept in Theresienstadt

Food items:

20 boxes of prunes 12.5 kilograms each net   250 kilograms
6 charitable packages each with

    3 packages of cookies
    1 package of oat flakes
    8 soup stock cubes
    1 package of marmalade
    3 packages meat
    1 tin Pritamin

200 boxes—4000 packages each with

    1 kilogram sugar
    1 package of vegetables
    1 rabbit pâté
    1 package cookies

18 boxes—424 packages each with

    1 package of ruga bread
    2 pieces of sausage
    1 piece of bacon
    1 can of milk
    1 package of oats
    1 tin of spices
    3 tins Ovaltine

100 cases—1800 packages, each containing

1 kilogram sugar
3 packages of cookies
1 package of cheese
1 tin of milk
20 cigarettes

104 boxes—1859 packages, each with

1 kilogram sugar
1 package of cheese
1 tin of milk
1 tin of sardines
2 packages of cookies

25 boxes—438 packages, each with

1 kilogram sugar
1 tin of milk
1 tin of sardines
1 tin of Ovaltine
1 gingerbread

4 boxes—62 packages, each with

2 kilogram sugar
1 package of cheese
1 gingerbread
1 tin of Pritamin
1 tube spice
40 cigarettes

250 boxes—4489 packages, each with

1 kilogram sugar
1 package of cheese
1 tin of milk
1 tin of sardines
2 packages of cookies

Outside of work it is not better either. So I decide from now on to go to the dentist regularly, in order to break up the long office hours. My tooth, which had given me quite a lot of pain for some time already, made day-long and very thorough visits to the dentist possible. Apart from that I also had—probably as a consequence of the unhealthy diet—all kinds of rashes. So I decided to—as one said at the camp—report myself as ill in order to stay healthy.

In order to be treated by a doctor one had to begin by obtaining an all-purpose certificate that entitled one to be on the street during office hours. It could happen that the SS would stop people in the streets during business hours. A certificate proving your identity was necessary to avoid being arrested then.

Theresienstadt had plenty of doctors.[25] In each district there was an infirmary in which different specialists held office hours side by side. In each office several doctors worked one right next to the other. As far as I could see, those infirmary rooms contained essential instruments and medicaments. Everything was damaged and ripped up by constant use, primitive and poor. But the doctors were good, and most of them took great care with their patients. Before the big transports to Auschwitz, there must not have been any other place in the whole world where so many outstanding specialists were working side by side in such restricted space. But then also many of those who helped humanity were sent to the gas chamber; doctors who were so scarce in other parts of the world were killed and so many people died because of a lack of medical care.

My infected tooth helped me get much free time. The dentist brushed it with cream again and again. The inflammation kept coming back. When it was nice outside—early spring was already in the air—I walked slowly across the city, but even when it rained I was never in a hurry. From the dentist I usually went to the dermatologist. I had reason enough. My skin was in a pitiful state. The doctor was a skeptical old Czech, who only shrugged his shoulders and suggested that in a few months I would get used to it. He had no interest, and I could not blame him for that. He also disliked Germans, for which I could not blame him either. He was only too familiar with such skin infections. Later I also went to the eye clinic several times, where a professor from

Prague University was tirelessly trying to help many patients with insufficient medical means.

One was, of course, never alone with the doctor during the sessions. The patients who were next in line were standing right next to one another, more or less undressed, according to each case. Since I am a curious person, I did not close my eyes when I saw emaciated bodies, ripped-up underwear, overused and mended up shirts and socks that consisted mostly of patches.

There were of course few possibilities for improvement or proper treatment for most of the illnesses, since the basic conditions for getting well were missing: rest, good care, and adequate nourishment. So for most, only a momentary alleviation could be achieved with the usual little remedies and potions. There were, of course, also complicated internal cases in which the cure depended exclusively on proper diagnosis by the doctor, cases in which the decisive factor was the genius and strength of the doctor and in which pure science was triumphant.

One received prescribed medication in small doses from the doctors. Thus, for instance, once the doctor prescribed me pills for a sore throat in a dose sufficient just for one day. Then one simply had to visit the doctor again. The small Dutch doctor, one of the most liked among the general practitioners, looked like a friendly Christmas gnome. He had a small goatee, sad blue eyes, and looked so hungry that he seemed ready to fall over. But he never became impatient, this little hungry man. He was a good little Jewish gnome. I remembered that once a patient had said to a very friendly family doctor, "Doctor, I should like to die in your establishment; it must be a pleasure to die here." The benevolent little man I describe surely inspired the same feeling.

For urgent cases there was a hospital, an old, unmodern hospital with wide stairs and giant rooms for the sick. Its arched ceilings made one think of a monastery. The means to help were limited here also. Some doctors were interested in helping, some were less so, like everywhere in the world. In February 1945, with liberation getting closer and closer, they knew well why they were working. But before that? There was little sense in curing somebody just to see him transported to Auschwitz afterward.[26]

12 March 1945

Today I found "Kanto." In reality, her name was quite different, of course. Only her friends called her Kanto. Kanto, Dr. Gertrud Kantorowicz, was once, in her civil life, a doctor of philosophy.[27] I knew that Kanto had tried to flee across the border to Switzerland, in the summer of 1942, together with a seventy-five-year old aunt, for whom she felt responsible, and several other elderly ladies. Kanto, courageous and fearless—according to her, she did not know what fear even meant— led the band of old Jewish ladies. Taking mountain paths, they intended in some way to get to Switzerland. However, precisely at that time a French general had escaped from German imprisonment; thus, the borders were being watched with especial care. Two of the five managed to cross the border and save themselves while gunshots were ringing out behind them. But Kanto and the other two only saw the Promised Land in front of them. Nothing of it! They were delivered to the prison in Bregenz. So Kanto with her old aunt Clara Kantorowicz ended up being brought to the women's prison in Bregenz on Lake Constance.[28] There they were interned with criminals of all kinds: thieves, whores, and similar rabble. Kanto, at the age of sixty-seven, had already secured a teaching position at a college in the USA, and her old aunt Clara Kantorowicz was the mother of a professor of history, Friedrich Kantorowicz, *who died in Princeton.*[29] In Bregenz, Kanto, who had a lively imagination and always knew how to transform the negative into the positive, started to tell stories and fairytales one evening in prison, because storytelling was one of her great skills. The way she could spin a yarn! Inspired by her stories, the other women started little by little to tell stories from their own lives, one after another. During those nights they could not get to sleep for a long time because it was too hot and sticky in the overcrowded rooms. Kanto and the other two refined Jewish ladies got to hear stories of a kind they had not heard before in their lives. Experiences of prostitutes, coquettes, burglars, and thieves. While one of the two elderly ladies was indignant at so much immorality, crime, and lewdness, Kanto's seventy-five-year aunt Clara simply said the next morning only, "This has been so far the most interesting night of my life."[30]

Kanto then came, in a roundabout way through many prisons, to Theresienstadt. When I saw her again, debilitated by many grave illnesses, she weighed barely eighty pounds. Her little round, intelligent head was framed by short white hair; she had only a few teeth left; her skin was blotchy. She was lying in her bed, her little mugs and bowls above her on a wooden plank, with her toiletries next to them, and she was reading Homer in the original Greek. Her brown eyes lit up when she saw me. She was working as an aid in a recovery home, on duty ten hours per day, and was constantly overworked by this physically demanding task. Once, when I visited her in the evening shortly after seven o'clock, her neighbor in the next bed was washing herself. There was of course almost always somebody in the room washing herself: one had to do it at a certain point. The young woman was stark naked. Kanto negotiated the unusual situation with the elegant gesture of a born lady, saying only, "Now I can introduce you to this lady, a philologist by profession, in a state that corresponds to her interest in the Greeks and their art—in the shape of Venus Anadyomene."

Kanto had received an additional ration of broth that evening. Because of their hazardous occupation, the employees of the hospitals used to be allotted a so-called hazard bonus portion. Thus, she handed me, the visitor, that cup of soup as a gift in a cup of real porcelain. It was the very first porcelain cup that I held in my hand. It was great luxury not to have to drink out of a marmalade jar or a tin cup for once. I myself had brought with me only aluminum dishes and an aluminum cup in order not to overload my baggage.

The many conversations I had with Kanto until her tragic death always followed a certain pattern. We always had barely ninety minutes. First, we usually commented on war developments. We both had a burning interest in every detail, no matter how small—in contrast to the majority of the other women who had only one interest: when will we be free? We discussed the pros and cons of all rumors in the camp. Kanto had a vivid vision of how the liberation would proceed. One day—she repeated again and again—the Czechs would take their own country back and the German dictatorship would disintegrate. Her predictions proved right. She herself did not live to see the liberation. An insidious case of meningitis carried her away fourteen days before the end. *(Kanto had a daughter who had emigrated to Israel. She spoke of her at times. Kanto never learned that her only child, who had lived in permanent fear of a deadly fall, actually died of a fall while working picking apples from a tree in a Kibbutz [Angela "Angi" Kantorowicz (1907-1944)].)*[31] But then we would abandon the present. It simply disappeared, and we passed on to subjects discussed across the world: art, politics, travel impressions, and encounters with people.

15 March 1945

Daily I grow more and more tired of the subjects perpetually discussed by the women in my room. This eternal gossip most often does not go beyond the simplest everyday subjects. Silly talk in every possible shape about every possible thing gets on my nerves. And this shallowness at a time when the fate of Europe was at stake. I felt I had to gather all my strength in order to survive the next days, weeks, and months without growing dull, apathetic, and tired of it all. Kanto, who had worked during the First World War as a nurse in a military hospital in Istanbul, only smiled at my complaints. "That kind of women's chatter is the same in all parts of the world. It is not different in any way from the small talk of the nurses back in Istanbul," she said to me.

Sixteen women in one room can only remain silent when they sleep. Otherwise, there is always something to be discussed. It is practically impossible to read even a few pages. If only they would chat in a low voice. But they are all so overexcited, frightened, and nervous that they are always bothering each other. I try frantically to read at least a few pages from Paula Modersohn's letters and diaries, in order to conjure a different world for a few minutes.[32] I plug my ears with my fingers. My bed—an upper-level bed—is near the only weak electric bulb. So I manage, with great effort, to decipher a few pages. When I arrive at the second page a bedbug drops right onto my book. By the time I reach the third page all the fifteen women have surrounded me in order to find out what I am reading. Grete, the blond laborer with the shrill Swabian voice, asked at once whether I would lend her the book, since she loved reading novels. It would have been too complicated to explain to her why these lyric diary notes of this turn-of-the-century painter would not meet her expectations. I suggested she should rather read *David Copperfield*, another book I had brought with me: there she would find more action than in Modersohn's meditations on the fine arts. Grete was not the only one who forgot about her own destiny for hours thanks to the worries and joys of little David Copperfield.

Almost everybody had brought one or two books they loved to the camp. Of course, these books made the rounds from one to another— that way each of us had always something to read.

There was also a lending library. It contained for the most part novels in other languages as well as scholarly books. It was created after the SS stole good and new furniture and furnishings from the apartments of the Jews, leaving behind only old stuff and objects that were useless to the SS.

15 March 1945

By pure chance the index card of an old friend of my parents from Berlin comes into my hands. The lady is living in the same Magdeburger barracks in which I work.

Every one of the eight huge army barracks was named after a city. So there was, for instance, next to the Magdeburger barracks, a Hamburger, a Dresdner, and a Hanover barracks. In the Magdeburger barracks there were quite a number of private lodgings in addition to the many offices. By the order of the SS, suddenly some special work had to be carried out during the night. So first of all, those living in the barracks would be wakened. Apart from employees of the office, some "prominent people" also lived there. My parents' old friend Elsa Strauss was one of the prominent people.[33]

The designation "prominent" was an invention of the SS. They decided who counted as "prominent." So there was a relative of a first lieutenant who could not save his Jewish sister-in-law from being deported to Theresienstadt but could arrange for her to live somewhat better than the others. There was also a former member of the Dutch-Indian Council [Emanuel Moresco (1869–1945)], one of the highest-ranking officials of the government in Holland.[34] There was an old

court actress, former friend and colleague of Emmi Göring.[35] There was
Martha [Mosse], the first female police superintendent in Prussia,
whose father [Albert Mosse] accepted an invitation in 1886 from the
Japanese government to work for it as an advisor. The list of the most
important laws, especially the new municipal code already in force, as
well as the district and provincial code ready for publication, derive
almost exclusively from his works. He was, apart from that, active in
almost all ministries as a trustworthy advisor on many matters. He
made an outstanding contribution to the official state constitution of
11 February 1889 and the state laws depending on it.[36] Around the turn
of the century he was sent to Japan by order of the German government
to establish a municipal and general internal plan for city administration on the German model. That man had an extraordinary reputation
in Japan, and his memory is venerated there even today.[37] On 1 April
1937, I, bearer of the same name, received a call from the Japanese em-
bassy in Berlin. A voice speaking in broken German asked me whether I
knew where the tomb of the great scholar Albert Mosse was. Two Japanese scholars wanted to go there and pray. I promised to try to find out
and to call back. Then I started to think about it. It was 1 April 1937:
Jews in Germany were being persecuted, ostracized, and chased. 1 April
of each year is the day on which everybody plays jokes and makes fun of
others. Was this an April fools' joke? But it was not an April fools' joke.
After finding out where the tomb was situated I called the Japanese em-
bassy and gave them the information. And the two traveling Japanese
scholars went to the tomb of the famous man, prayed there, and left a
wreath. By intervention of the Japanese government Albert's daughter
was then declared "prominent" in Theresienstadt.

Also among the prominent people were the former mayor of the
French city Le Havre [Léon Meyer (1868–1948)], a state prosecutor
from Berlin, the widow [Ida Franziska Schneidhuber (1892–1978)] of
Munich's former police director [August Schneidhuber (1887–1934)]
who played a part in the Roehm affair. Another person declared prominent was Elsa Bernstein, a writer who had published dramas, tragedies,
stories, and poems under the name Ernst Rosmer.[38] Her fairytale comedy

The Children of the King had been adapted by [Engelbert] Humperdinck [1854–1921] for a musical piece. In 1945 this blind woman turned seventy-nine years old. Altogether there were some three hundred prominent people. They lived like a poor maid who has saved a few thousand marks throughout her entire life and has to end her life in an institution for poor old people.

In Martha's room, where she lived together with the first lieutenant's sister-in-law, the ambience was as follows.

The room had one window, and its walls were painted a bright color—a seldom seen luxury. There were two beds that were transformed into sofas during the day, two wardrobes, an old-fashioned chest of drawers for linens, a table, and four hard chairs. All this furniture was of poor quality and in bad taste and had been discarded by the SS. A simple lamp with a weak bulb hung from the ceiling in the center of the room. On two wooden stools there were two enamel basins. The tap was in the corridor, next to the toilet—one of only two appliances with flowing water that I saw in Theresienstadt. This poorly furnished room was one of the most beautiful rooms in all of Theresienstadt.[39] It was situated in one of the few newer houses in town. Martha and her roommate, a friendly elderly lady from Hanover, with wonderfully bright white hair, were scrubbing and cleaning all the time in order to keep the room free of bedbugs.

My parents' old friend Elsa Strauss was the widow of a respected specialist in internal medicine, Professor Hermann Strauss from Berlin.[40] She lived with Trude Zülzer, an old painter.[41] The two ladies shared a large room and had their own kitchen, which led to an inner path around the barracks that was lined with trees. We had an emotional reunion. She had visited my mother after I was born and looked after me back then. She had already been living in the camp for three years. Her husband had died very suddenly six months earlier of a heart attack. His death saved him and his wife from a transport of people destined for extermination in Auschwitz, for which his name was already entered in the lists. The name of his widow was removed from the lists; she never found out that she had been listed for extermination. *She did*

Trude Zülzer painted this image of Eva Noack-Mosse in June 1945. Eva later recalled, "As payment she received a jam jar filled with oatmeal (=160 grams)." ("Also miscellaneous personal documents including Jewish identity card," p. 2, Wiener Library Document 504d/1)

not live to see freedom either. She became sickly and wilted like a flower without water. She died three weeks before transportations back to Berlin began.

The two old ladies had just received orders from an institution with the high-sounding name "Living Quarters Administration" that was responsible for dividing up and distributing the inhabitants of the camp. The two had to make room for a third person in their smoky old kitchen because many more newcomers were expected.

We agreed right away that I would move into that kitchen. We devised a proper attack plan and way to implement it, since I was not a prominent person, and officially prominent and nonprominent people were not permitted to live together.

Though they were sent together to Auschwitz and Poland to be exterminated by gas, special tricks were necessary to arrange for prominent and nonprominent people to live together in Theresienstadt. So I spoke with a lady in the Living Quarters Administration. Like me she was from Berlin. She came to understand immediately during our first conversation that I was prepared to give her something in return for her readiness to help: a charitable package Mrs. Strauss had received, plus two weekly rations of sugar, which I had saved. After some negotiations, which the lady from Berlin undertook with her Czech superior, I was allowed to move into room 117c in the Magdeburg barracks.

17 March 1945

I am scrubbing the kitchen, and I shall be able to move in today. The walls of that kitchen were black from smoke. The grated window looked out onto the inner path around the barracks, an open yard. Almost always it was so dark that one had to have the light on. The toilet was in the room across from the kitchen: an old, not always clean, toilet. In the kitchen, next to an ancient coal stove, there was an old-fashioned kitchen cupboard with many superfluous ornaments, a chest of drawers in the same style, a table, three cases of coal, and two kitchen chairs. The old wooden floor was black as coal. Since the old doctor's widow was too weak for any housework, and the old painter very kind but also terribly disorderly, I had to roll up my sleeves and indulge in a cleaning spree. Then I got myself an old plank bed and went to the mattress collection center, which was run by an old gardener from Hanover. I gave him two thick slices of bread. Bread was equal to cash, since the official camp money was good for nothing. For those two slices of bread he found me a good mattress and carried it all the way to my kitchen. After scrubbing for hours, the black floor started showing some dark gray spots. I had to carry out countless buckets of black water. Countless layers of dirt had to be scrubbed away. Since the two old ladies were too weak for scrubbing floors, an old man came to help them two times a week. They could not afford to pay him bread more than twice a week.

One has to bring water from the well in the courtyard or from a laundry which is so far away that one prefers to go out to the courtyard, even when it is raining. Down in the yard is also where the food distribution point is for the entire barracks and the surrounding quarters. So from now on I don't have to go far to fetch my food. I'll be able to warm it up in my kitchen. This is the beginning of a new way of life.

18 March 1945

Great surprise in my old room when I tell them that I am moving. They don't actually understand why I am going to move. I don't want to offend my roommates: in their own way, they have always been very kind to me. Of course, I cannot explain to them that their daily, ever-repeated, tiresome chatter exhausts me and little by little is robbing me of strength that I absolutely need. I simply could not bear any longer to hear the same question every day: "When are we going home?" I long to be able to undress by myself in the evening. A new tin basin destined for me alone is beckoning at my new quarters.

From now on I don't have to appear at the roll call every evening, in which the house superior, that little thin man with the sad eyes, exhorts us every time that we have to keep the toilet clean and warns us not to put on any light during air raids, among other things. In the Magdeburg barracks no such appeals were made. The house administration posted all announcements on blackboards.

In half an hour I packed my bag and knapsack, pulled out the hooks I had put into the wall to hang my belongings, and happily moved into my new quarters. The two old ladies received me with emotion. For Mrs. Strauss, I was a piece of the living past. She had lived for years just a few houses away from us at old Kurfürstendamm across from the zoo, where Theodor Fontane's [1819-1898] novel *Trials and Tribulations* takes place. Her children, both my sisters, and I had played marbles together in the zoo, accompanied by nannies, as was customary at the time. For Trude Zülzer, I was a new friend connected to her earlier world by many threads.

These two old ladies protected me as a daughter. For both, I became a daughter and a friend at the same time.

20 March 1945

Finally, today once again news from the front. The Allied forces are advancing more rapidly. Accordingly, our mood is improving.

I am helping the old ladies, bringing them water, washing their dishes. The old painter—the cook in our trio—has warmed up my food and embellishes the tiresome, daily, mediocre potatoes with some tricks. She loves to make herself busy around the old stove, and like many other women in the camp, with practically nothing she transforms the awful camp food into something edible. I enjoy sleeping by myself enormously. I have peace; quiet reigns in my dark kitchen when nothing is being cooked.

Up until the spring of 1945, Mrs. Strauss regularly received charitable parcels from Denmark and Sweden. Every morning she cooked a large pot of soup, and around ten o'clock, when the soup was ready, a small group of visitors would arrive. Everyone received a dish of good, nourishing barley or millet soup. I quickly absconded from the office, ran the one hundred steps to the kitchen, and daily saved an entire portion of bread through this, my second breakfast. This meant a lot.

22 March 1945

Today it is a month since I arrived at the camp. Time passes incredibly slowly. Every new day is a new problem to be solved. When there is good news from the front the day passes quickly and without pain. When the advancing front gets stuck or we hear nothing new, the day is hard and difficult. I have no news from home. Surely my husband does not know yet where he should look for me in his thoughts. Did he receive the cards I mailed while I was on the way? Is the eldest daughter still with the antiaircraft artillery in Westphalia? The curtain separating me from home is getting ever thicker, heavier, and more impervious. What is happening at home?

All my colleagues at the office claim in unison that my hair has already grown much longer and that I can now think of getting a modern hairdo. I admire these women, who begin each gray day by relentlessly trying to make themselves as pretty as possible. What toughness: to find patience, to invent ways with such insufficient means to produce pretty locks. Actually, the locks were just a symbol of many other values: the importance of taking care of oneself, of making oneself pretty, of pretending things were otherwise. This was comforting. It had deeper meaning.

I found a new friend at the food distribution center, a south German. Her only daughter lives in Sweden. She hopes to get to Sweden one day and to be able to take greetings to my friends there. She is already looking forward to that. For the moment she shows her affection by giving me daily seconds, three extra-large potatoes daily—the most beautiful thing one could receive.

Little by little we all come to know it, we feel it: in a few months we'll see the end of the Third Reich, provided that we are still alive. Many still fear that we might get deported before that, since the rail tracks to Mauthausen-Linz are still not in the hands of the Allies. What we do know about Mauthausen, since we have people here who were there before: Mauthausen is one of the most horrible concentration camps that exists—hence the name "Mordhausen" [site of murders] that it has acquired generally.

24 March 1945

The old painter has put on my bed an old, well-thumbed copy of Gottfried Keller's Zurich novellas. When I am alone I am not disturbed by the banging of the toilet door across from me, the perpetual clickety-clack of the steps in the hallways until late at night, or the shrill voices in the yards. These are far-away noises that do not affect me. On my bed lays my checkered plaid, which I brought from home. Every morning, when I spread it over my bed, I think: "If suddenly my husband came into this old kitchen full of smoke, he would recognize the plaid and realize that I live here."

25 March 1945

The first air raid alarm. In the middle of the day. We lie on the broad window planks of the barracks and look out for the airplanes. We know very well that no Allied plane will bomb Theresienstadt. The contour of the fortified city is so clearly recognizable that no mistake is possible. We all feel very secure. The alarm lasts a long time, past the noon break. Nobody may go out onto the street. Thus, the noon break gets longer. All are happy about it. Hopefully, the planes will come really often from now on.

26 March 1945

Little by little I get an overview of the statistical records, both of the number of camp inhabitants and of the transports to Poland.

The number of people living in Theresienstadt fluctuated. The highest number was 62,000. In total, about 135,000 people passed through Theresienstadt.[42] These were mostly elderly people whose children had emigrated believing that their parents would die in peace in their own country. This explains the large number of "natural" deaths. Thirty-five thousand, mostly old people, died in Theresienstadt within forty months. Ninety thousand were transported further East—to Poland, to Auschwitz, and other places of extermination. A small portion of these ninety thousand went to the Reich on so-called worker transports. Out of these ninety thousand only a very low percentage have survived. In the summer of 1944 there were some twenty-eight thousand inhabitants. Of these twenty-eight thousand, in September and October 1944 some eighteen thousand went East: two-thirds of the total number of inhabitants. This was the last real horror the inhabitants had to live through. In January 1945 the Russian offensive made further transports to Poland impossible.

Converted to percentages, a little more than 7 percent survived the deportation to Theresienstadt, 67 percent went on to Poland, Auschwitz, and the "worker transports," 26 percent died a natural death—that is, died owing to a loss of strength or succumbed to an epi-demic or illness that most of them would have overcome under normal circumstances.[43]

In the period of the great epidemics in 1942 and 1943 some two to three hundred persons died daily.[44] The worst epidemic was the ty-phoid outbreak in the spring of 1943. Most of the older people did not survive very long after deportation. They became weaker and weaker and died when they were struck by the first illness. During the period of the great epidemics there were practically no beds or mattresses available; medicines were a rarity. The ill people were lying in heaps on the floor. Knapsacks and coats served as pillows; a washbasin was a coveted luxury. It was practically impossible to find chlorine for disinfection; a piece of paper was as precious as a nugget of gold. But those who survived the first months developed an astounding toughness. The elderly especially demonstrated a striking will to live. Yearning and hope kept many alive. *(See the note in the preface regarding small inaccuracies in the statistics.)*

And they were starving. Their nourishment consisted of soups made with water in which now and then a little piece of a halfway cooked potato was swimming. Now and then, intermittently, there came a small piece of bread. One has to be careful with the expression "starving," but in this case one can say that hundreds and even thousands died of hunger.[45] Perhaps not in the literal sense of the word. There are so many stages of hunger, from not having had enough to eat to the light gnawing in the stomach area to a spasm and headache, until one has but one de-sire: to appease one's hunger—one does not want anything else, there can be nothing more wonderful in the whole world. Those people did not die of hunger, but they kept losing weight rapidly and thus lost re-sistance to the point that often they became victims of an intestinal catarrh. They were dying like flies. Within the first year four of my eight relatives died that way. They were elderly, but they had been relatively healthy when they left Berlin. They were already rather thin when they arrived in Theresienstadt, since from 1941 on food rations for Jews had been reduced in all of Germany. They did not receive even a drop of skimmed milk, nor meat, nor white bread or white flour. They only re-ceived some very common vegetables once a week, like rutabaga, cab-bage, or beets.[46]

On 5 February 1945 a transport of twelve hundred Jews left Theresienstadt for Switzerland. Those who had been earmarked for the Swiss transportation went in decent second-class rail coaches, and they received good, sufficient food for the trip. The SS even gave them vitamin supplements for the trip, after they had eaten nothing containing vitamins until then.[47] And they were told to report in Switzerland that they "had always lived pretty decently in Theresiensatadt." All this in spite of the fact that during all their stay in Theresienstadt they had not seen any butter, milk, nor fresh fruit or vegetables, nor eggs or fish. Did the SS really believe that nobody in Switzerland would talk about the actual circumstances?

Of course, as a consequence of malnutrition there were all kinds of deficiency diseases, a lot of tuberculosis, and a softening of the bones. Due to a lack of phosphorus, all inhabitants suffered from lack of memory. Women ceased to have regular menstruation periods—a phenomenon known to the doctors to be a consequence of being in prison or in concentration camps. Because of vitamin deficiency rheumatic illnesses could not be healed. Cases of tuberculosis became grave because of lack of milk and butter. It is true that in later years some fat free milk for the sick became available, but it was a drop in the ocean.

Children received some supplements. I cannot say anything exact about the number of children. *According to statistics, on 13 May 1945 there were among the Reichsdeutschen 307 children and youths under nineteen years old, which amounted to 6 percent of the total population.*[48] *This number should be more or less indicative of the total. In my experience, the percentages within a single group tended to reflect the entire population of the camp.*

Children represented a society apart.[49] At the beginning, in 1941, they separated men and women, parents and children. Each group lived separately in mass accommodations. Small children were in turn separated from bigger ones. There was no family life. Spouses could converse in the evenings. Sometime later, some of the parents moved in together and took the bigger children with them.[50] Small children were better off in the primitive kindergartens, since the parents had to work and could not take care of them.

Study and any kind of teaching was strictly forbidden by the SS. Violations were punished the same way as everything else in Theresienstadt: by deportation, that is to say, death. In spite of this, many grown-ups tried to get around this frightful prohibition against teaching. There were many musicians, teachers, and pedagogues very eager to transmit something useful to the children.[51] It was unbearable to see one's children illiterate. This was a well-planned de-education intended to return Jews to the small Jewish peddler of a medieval ghetto. Besides, all those children were destined, sooner or later, for the gas chamber.[52] But before that, they had to live degraded and ostracized, as pariahs excluded from all that was beautiful and good in a cultivated world. This was part of the SS plan. It would have been more merciful to have shot them right away instead of taking away all their rights little by little and consciously tormenting them over ten years. And when they died, their golden teeth were torn out and their hair sold, all in order to reduce the deficit of the German Empire.

Valiant teachers and people made the children visit them secretly. The children had the desire to learn. There was, for instance, a former high school teacher who made some children go to her house several times a week for history lessons. The children knew exactly what they had to say in case an SS man suddenly appeared in the room.

Since the children did not have regular classes and were deliberately cut off from all culture and education, most of them were used in the offices as errand runners. Older boys went to the workshops as apprentices. In this way, they saw and heard things that were not at all appropriate for them all day long; they became precociously wise, turned into pessimists, and started their "businesses" too soon. Their lives were focused on bartering.

In these circumstances, there was great temptation to commit petty thefts. *A fourteen-year old boy from Berlin, half Jewish, was summoned to the magistrate for investigation in April 1945. During the hearing, it was discovered that he had been a member of the Hitlerjugend in Berlin.[53] When restrictions concerning half Jews were tightened he was expelled from the Hitlerjugend. He came to Theresienstadt. A little before the liberation he heard soon he would be able to go back to Berlin. He believed that now he had to "make his way" one way or the other to Berlin and stole a water faucet from a plumber. This seemed to him better than not having any weapon at all . . .*

These children did not know any animals. It was forbidden to have pets. The only animals I saw were two oxen working in the fields. The industrial farming took place outside the city walls. Only agricultural workers were permitted to go there.

What will these children eventually become? On the one hand, they are so far behind in matters of science and knowledge that according to school standards they are practically illiterate; on the other hand, they have seen and experienced more than some who have lived for seventy long years. There is such a great lag between knowledge and experience in their case that the scales are completely out of balance.

A portion of them went from Theresienstadt where they vegetated — this condition did not deserve to be called life — to the East: to Auschwitz, to Birkenau, to Gleiwitz, and other places of horror. But even there not all the children were exterminated right away. Even Auschwitz, the site of a million deaths, had a "kindergarten." I spoke to a lady who had worked in a "kindergarten" of this kind in Auschwitz.

Among the younger women who worked in my office, four had become widows in Theresienstadt; the husbands of another four had been taken in autumn 1944 on a so-called workers' transport. *Most of these "workers' transports" went to the German Reich. There, these slaves were put to work in the arms industry. Since working conditions and nourishment were inhuman there, only a very few survived such torture. Out of the four husbands of my work comrades only one returned home alive.*

In general, men suffered more, both bodily and spiritually, than did women. They were exposed to more intense hunger; even when their wives gave them a part of the pitiful food they received, it was not enough to satisfy their hunger. They were less resistant. They contracted and died from diseases which the tougher women withstood. They had greater difficulty in adjusting; they suffered more from the change in their lives. So, for instance, a lawyer suffered terribly from the fact that he had become a street sweeper, more than a woman, formerly a chemist, who now worked in the laundry.

Three times as many men as women died from the typhus epidemic, which produced many victims during the last months. Among the 5,500 *Reichsdeutschen* who remained alive and left the camp at the time of the liberation there were twice as many women than men, 774 men over sixty one years old, compared to 1,531 women in the same age range.[54]

The number of camp inhabitants fluctuated. After the deportation of eighteen thousand in autumn of 1944 the ghetto was replenished with around five thousand new mixed marriage persons and children of mixed-race couples. Because of the approaching Russians, roughly fifteen hundred Hungarians from a Hungarian camp and also some smaller camps of Slovaks were moved to Theresienstadt. Thus the number of inhabitants increased to seventeen thousand by the end of March 1945.[55] *To this, on 20 April 1945—that is, just before the end of the war—a further twelve thousand detainees from various German and Austrian concentration camps, mostly Hungarians and Poles, were added.[56] I shall discuss them later.*

Among those seventeen thousand inhabitants there were sixty-two hundred Czechs, five thousand *Reichsdeutsche*, thirteen hundred Austrians, thirteen hundred Dutch, fourteen hundred Slovaks, eleven hundred Hungarians.[57] The rest were of various nationalities. There were Swedes and Argentinians, Peruvians and Turks, US citizens and Rumanians, Greeks and Italians, Lithuanians, English citizens, Russians, and citizens of Honduras. I leafed through the lists, and found people deported from Rhodes, from Oslo, from Crimea and from Salonika, from Smolensk and Tunis, from Bucharest and Marseille, from Algiers and Riga, from Copenhagen and Bordeaux, from Athens and Lyon, from Budapest and Kiev. Since a good part of them were not pure-blood Jews, and some of them had husbands or wives who were Catholic, Christian, Greek Orthodox, etc., there were only eleven thousand inhabitants of Jewish faith among the seventeen thousand.[58]

And how many SS men were there to supervise them? We calculated around a few hundred.[59] Some of them lived in modern rebuilt houses. Of course, the houses in which the SS men and their families resided were very strictly separated from the other houses. It was forbidden for the Jews to enter those streets. There were guards on each corner. The SS lodgings were provided with all the modern comforts; there was a small park with a swimming pool constructed by Jews—reserved for the wives and children of the SS. They received what the

Jews cultivated in their exemplary, organized farming. The SS always had fresh vegetables and wonderful fruit in this fertile land. A settlement was bought in the vicinity of the town with Jewish money. The SS men and their families had the exclusive right to dispose of what this would produce. It was strictly forbidden for the Jews to eat even the smallest portion of the vegetables and fruit that they reaped. A young woman who had thrown a pear over the wall to her husband was taken to Auschwitz as a punishment.

The SS headquarters were located in the former townhouse on the market square. No Jew was allowed to set foot on that side of the market square.

When it got dark—and because it was wartime all lights were shaded—a very clear light on the corner of the market square came on. Its cold light illuminated the empty side of the square. Only those who had business to do with the SS office were allowed to cross over to that side and enter the building. Since the SS had many desires, and those desires had to be immediately satisfied by the Jewish slaves, there was always a lively hustle and bustle around that house. Sometimes an inhaler was needed for an SS commander who had a cold. A Jew had to run across to the pharmaceutical depot and obtain an inhaler for the commander and bring it to him. Since I worked in the office where the wishes of the SS came in by phone, I heard all those wishes. Herr Obersturmführer [Karl Rahm] wanted a new down bedcover.[60] One brought him samples of the available materials. The night shift had to work without interruption, and the following morning he had the desired bedcover. Of the best quality, of course. Herr Obersturmführer was very spoiled. All kinds of repairs had to be carried out immediately. An army of craftsmen was always at his disposal. New electrical lines were introduced, damage to the roof repaired, curtains to shut out the light at night mended or replaced, new wallpaper put up, stoves moved. Ah, there were so many wishes. It was like in a fairytale for the SS in Theresienstadt during the war. A mass of slaves under their command ready to fulfill any wish.

There was a period of time when women were forbidden to get pregnant while they were in the camp.[61] Only those who were already pregnant when they arrived were allowed to give birth. Women who became pregnant in spite of this rule came into terrible difficulties. They hoped that by the time they would be ready to give birth the war would have ended and the Third Reich vanished. But so often after a few months, they came to realize that their child would be born within the Third Reich. And that the child would have to disappear.[62] In later years this restriction was abolished.

One of the worst crimes was smoking and smuggling uncensored letters out of the camp. Seventeen persons were once hanged publicly on the market square for this offense.[63] Since there was no professional hangman, the community was ordered to find one among the Jews. If this type of person could not be found the community council itself would have to carry out the order. Fortunately—in such a case it is justified to say "fortunately"—a half-crazy butcher was found who was a real drunkard. He hanged the seventeen Jews. The SS men [Karl] Bergel and [Rudolf] Heindl were standing at the side smoking cigarettes.[64] Herr Heindl did show a stirring of humanity when he shot a man who was still breathing with his pistol after seeing that he was not quite dead yet.[65]

1 April 1945

Stories, stories, and more stories in the office. Almost all the women in my office have been here for four years already. Since Czechs were the first inhabitants, they went through the worst times.[66] Now, so they tell me again and again, all is arranged in a much better way. It is possible now to move freely and to speak on the street. There are concerts, there are church services for all confessions. No regular religious services of course, only those that fit the prescriptions of the SS. Still, they are religious services. Concerts and other similar entertainments became part of the artificial life the Jews were now allowed to live. Some people wrote about this to their friends and relatives. Since they were not allowed to mention the fear in which they constantly lived, nor to write about all those who had died or been transported to Poland, since it was forbidden even to mention any desire, what was there to write about? It is human nature to try not to cause unnecessary worries for loved ones.

This explains why people who were starving and living in constant fear of being included in the next transport to extermination could heroically write to their relatives and friends: "We are in good health; we even have concerts here."

People lived like puppets. The SS held all the strings in their hands. Whenever they let the strings of a person drop this meant deportation, death, the end. Off!

2 April 1945

Fulda has been conquered by the Allies; this means they are now in the center of Germany.

Yesterday twenty-nine "submarines" arrived with a transport from Berlin. Submarines are "submerged" people who had been living without valid personal documentation.[67] *In all of the German cities, the army was carrying out large raids looking for deserted soldiers. Thousands were fed up with slaughtering and risking their lives for Hitler and were deserting. The army undertook raids. Streetcars would be surrounded and checked; all those inside had to show their identity cards. In these raids many Jews who were living without valid documents and who had not registered were arrested at the eleventh hour, imprisoned, and held for many weeks until new mass transports could be organized. Their prison cells were not opened during air raid sirens. They could not go to air raid shelters. If a bomb landed on the building, fire would break out—in fact, many fires did break out—so the prisoners were abandoned to their horrible destiny. How many burned alive during those air attacks?*

Among the twenty-nine new "submarines" there was a young man from Berlin who had lived "submerged" for three years. Although during the last six weeks in Berlin he had lived only in prisons, he was very well informed about everything: prices of food items, news transmitted by Allied radio stations, the scarcity of potatoes, prices on the black market, and much more worth knowing. Of course, people from Berlin could not get enough news. They were gulping down his reports like travelers through the desert who had their first drink of water after an odyssey.

To celebrate the young man from Berlin, I share my little bag of dried apples. Since it is Easter everyone also receives a piece of bread that tastes like gingerbread—a specialty of Czech cuisine. After that, we eat our evening potato soup. We all sit together in Martha's little simple room, forget all that is surrounding us, and those of us who were born in Berlin spend hours talking about that abused city that endures it all with such nonchalance and boldness.[68]

3 April 1945

Once more, the rumor is spreading that in a few days an International Commission will visit the camp. Besides that, a young pale SS man appeared in the office today and asked to be shown and told everything— evidently he was seeking to determine whether there might be any undesirable files and papers in the offices. The Potemkin villages have to be reconstructed for another inspection.[69] We all get very excited by the prospect of a new inspection by a foreign commission. It is not the first inspection carried out by foreigners.

It all started in the summer of 1944 when, for the first time, an International Commission visited the ghetto.[70] During the months before, the Jewish town was beautified for this purpose. The ugly tents were cleared from town hall square where the seventeen Jews had been hanged and where afterward work was carried out for the German war machine. Seeds for a green lawn were sown; it grew rather quickly thanks to the favorable climate and soon started looking like a real lawn. Paths with benches were introduced, a music pavilion was erected, a band formed— as if this were a spa town. A playground for the children to play in was erected, as well as a covered hall—it gave the impression that the children habitually played there when the weather was bad. Flowerbeds sprang up; wooden carved and hand-painted signposts appeared everywhere. A dining pavilion was constructed, with new tables and stools built at the carpenter's workshop. In the houses where people were living, special days and weeks for cleaning were established. During these weeks, all those living there had to be fully dressed by seven in the morning, in case the building might be inspected. On the patios, even the smallest pile of dirt disappeared. Curtains were distributed for the duration of the inspection. Washed clothes were allowed to be hung for drying in the rooms only in the evening when there was no more fear that an inspector might appear. The impression of a clean and well-tended place had to be created. Backpacks, sacks with dirty clothes, etc. that hung on the walls had to disappear and be hidden in dark corners. Curtains were put in front of the wooden stands in which people kept cooking pots, little bowls, combs, brushes, bread, lard, and whatever else they had. The sidewalks were swept, cleaned, and sprinkled with water. We were told to use only the roads for walking so the sidewalks would stay clean until the day of the inspection. Menus promising wonders were printed. Unfortunately, one got to see those wonders only on the days on which the inspection team came. The following day there remained nothing of what the printed leaflet had announced so boastfully but instead just the usual potato or barley soup. In the hospitals—the favorite location of every inspection—there was much ado for many weeks before. In front of the used towels clean ones were hung that no one was allowed to use. For days, taking X-rays was forbidden in order to prevent dirt from being brought into the rooms. Old, ugly, sickly persons were not allowed on the street on the days of the inspection. The children at the kindergarten were instructed to run with welcoming smiles to meet the Obersturmführer Rahm and the International Commission and to shout "How wonderful, dear uncle Rahm, that you are visiting us again."

All the stores were put in order and the window displays filled with wonderful things that unfortunately were not for sale. In the linen stores in particular, the most wonderful and beautiful items, all of which had been confiscated from the Jews at their arrival, were put on display. In the only grocery of the town, instead of the usual herb infusions and spices entire pyramids of fat and sugar, unfortunately not for sale, were piled up. In short, an enormous web of lies was spun.

Every inhabitant received instructions to avoid answering inquiries from members of the commission until a specially instructed group leader could reply. In case one could not avoid answering for some reason, one had to reply, if possible: "I do not know." Since everywhere there was an SS man present no one had the courage to give an honest answer anyway.

They were producing a film, which was to show—in this way—how the Jews were living. According to rumor, it was to be titled *Hitler Gives the Jews a City*. Nobody knows what became of that movie, but it was made. *(Many years later the producer of that movie was taken to court in Czechoslovakia and heavily punished.)*[71]

The Jewish elders, who had to take the lead, knew that they were not allowed to say a single unauthorized word while talking to the foreign commission. The SS stood behind them, watching.

They made such an artificial show of it that in Theresienstadt, where there had never been room for jokes, many people were quipping about those Potemkin villages. Everyone was mocking the theater in the kindergarten and cracking jokes about how the children should shout out to the leader of the SS "Uncle Rahm": "Are you bringing sardines again? We have stuffed ourselves with them." Sardines from a charity parcel were the dream of all inhabitants. From time to time a tin of sardines could also be found in parcels coming from the Red Cross. The lucky owner of such a tin of sardines was immensely envied. A tin of sardines was an umbrella term for anything that was beautiful and desirable.

The summer 1944 inspection had been successful. At least according to the SS. Everything had been perfectly prepared, and the International Commission let the SS throw sand into its eyes. Only one thing could not be ordered, and it was so important for making a good impression: nice weather. If the weather was fine, one could sprinkle the unpaved streets so that they would not be too dusty. If it rained, the muddy soil almost instantly turned into a sticky black substance. On the day of the inspection, a light rain started just before noon and lasted through the entire afternoon.

Ever since that inspection in July 1944 everybody had dreamed of the possibility that Theresienstadt would come under the protection of the International Red Cross. Naturally, nobody had any exact information; they only heard rumors. There was, however, the fact, the naked fact, that the commission had come and that the SS had watched carefully to ensure that not a single unpermitted word would be spoken. Or could the Jewish elder who was responsible [Dr. Paul Eppstein] have said something that was not allowed or used an unobserved moment to give the commission some material? We do not know, and we shall never find out, since the elder who sacrificed himself for the community was handed over to the Gestapo shortly after the inspection and was never seen again.[72]

4 April 1945

A woman working in the ceramic workshop told us that for several weeks she has been making urns for an artificial grove. For the inspection, an artificial cemetery had to be created. Because what would one show to the members of the high commission if it occurred to them to inquire about the whereabouts of thirty-five thousand dead persons?

So the ceramic workshop received an order to produce 120 urns for a kind of "grove of honor." The construction department was ordered to deliver a tombstone with patina. All seems to be in perfect order again.

What became of the ashes of the thirty-five thousand dead?[73] *In September 1944, after the commission visit, and after sending eighteen thousand unfortunate persons to the East, the SS ordered that all files and any other trace of the dead and those deported be systematically and thoroughly destroyed. The ashes, conserved in numbered card boxes, were handed over to the SS, and we are probably not wrong to assume that the remains of the thirty-five thousand dead were thrown into the nearby river [Elbe River].*

The rumor has spread that the commission is really here today. We are excited; only the skeptics among us shake their heads and say, "They were here once before already; nothing came of it; after the inspection, another eighteen thousand people were sent East."

Be that as it may, the sign reading "Women" is torn down from the prehistoric toilet opposite my kitchen so that it will not occur to the commission making its rounds to have a closer look at this room. Most toilets in my barracks were simply locked for the duration of the inspection, since they were not "up to inspection standards."

Anyway, we are all looking forward to some good food and to enjoying the charity parcels that are being hastily distributed: cookies, sugar, sixty grams of cheese per person. These were the offerings of the Swiss Red Cross. The commission was supposed to see that the SS really distributed those parcels. We had no idea how long these gifts had been stacked away.

6 April 1945

The commission is really here. It inspects the city and its facilities, led by some SS men. We stuff ourselves with vegetable soup made from

Swiss donations and meatballs. Of course, we do not learn what is being negotiated or what is at stake. The rumor that the camp will come under the protection of the International Red Cross has again seeped through all of the cracks and canals. For us, the Red Cross is the embodiment of humanity, of justice, and of compassion. The parcels distributed among us—the commission has brought several more truckloads—are not just sugar, cookies, and cheese. They are the greeting of a good world, a world that has not forgotten about us.

7 April 1945

We receive news about the occupation of Hanover by the Allies. Accordingly, we are in a good mood. Everything seems to be advancing at a good pace. Of course, never quickly enough for us. We would have preferred to stand behind the armies and push every single Allied soldier forward.

I now understand why the offices constantly double-check and count anew how many inhabitants there are in the camp. During one control count of the number of inhabitants in 1943 a difference of five persons was discovered.[74] Afterward, all inhabitants in groups of one hundred were led on a cold, wet November day onto a wet grass field, the so-called Bauchowitzer Kessel, a low-lying terrain between Theresienstadt and the village of Bauchowitz. Twenty-seven thousand Jews in groups of one hundred stood on the field for the whole day without moving, without being allowed to move. It was 11 November 1943. All were expecting to be shot; they had resigned themselves to dying. No one moved or spoke in a loud voice. On that day—this is what all those who had been there told me—the Jews had stood the test, just as the best among them had expected they would. With dignity and self-control they awaited what would come, death or life. Silent as a herd of cattle they stood there on the meadow. In the evening, the SS announced that all could go home.[75]

No one knows what the SS thinks now that the war situation has changed. A newly trained police dog was tested on Jews just the other day. The unlucky person had to stand still. The dog was set on him; they wanted to test whether the dog would obey the orders of the SS.

Two Jews served for this exercise because the first one was injured in the process.

The following story illustrates the SS way of thinking. Only a few days before the final withdrawal an SS man saw a strong young woman engaged in difficult manual labor in the waterworks. Since autumn 1944, after the greater part of the young men fit for work had been taken to the Reich in transports destined for armament factories, many women were engaged in heavy work. The SS man observed the hard-working woman, asked her for her name, and said, "Should the Jew get the upper hand after all and win this war, I'll see to it that you receive a bonus and are included among the first to be sent to Switzerland." If we analyze this sentence part by part, the following train of thought of the SS is revealed:

a) For the SS man, victory by the Allies meant victory by Jews.
b) In spite of victory by the Allies the SS man presumes that he will still have the right to have his say and be able to determine which Jews ought to be rewarded.

This is how the SS man's mind pictured the world. *But the following document illustrates how the thinking and common sense of long-time detainees in the ghettoes had been influenced as well. This letter was issued to me by the director of our office on 28 May 1945, that is, twenty days after the capitulation. By order of the SS the office was designated "Jewish Self-Administration Theresienstadt":*

(letterhead printed)
Jewish Self-Administration Theresienstadt
Population Department
Central Evidence

Certificate

Mrs. Eva Noack, transportation no. 1379-II/34, born on 25 June 1902 in Berlin, in Theresienstadt since 22 February 1945, at present living at Theresienstadt, Hauptstraße 22/117, was employed as typewriter of the

Central Evidence office without interruption from 25 February 1945 until the present day.

The said person has given proof of excellence during the entire time of her work at the Central Evidence office and carried out the tasks assigned to her conscientiously and to our entire satisfaction.

We wish her much luck and success in the future.

Zentralevidenz

Director

Dr. Hermann Weiss

Theresienstadt, 28 May 1945

One of the most unbearable prohibitions for men was the prohibition against smoking.[76] The SS confiscated all smoking material from unsuspecting new arrivals. No one knew how many of these confiscated goods were then secretly sold back to the Jews at astronomical prices. At any rate, the smuggling of cigarettes was widespread. In February 1945, two cigarettes were worth half a loaf of bread, that is, the bread ration for three days. Some of the men were so crazy for cigarettes that they would go hungry in order to obtain two of them. Unconfirmed rumors said that this smuggling was secretly fostered by the SS. One cigarette came to cost up to twenty deutsche marks.[77] According to the law, one was not allowed to be in possession of those twenty deutsche marks: apart from the currency used in the ghetto possession of money was strictly forbidden. From time to time, whoever was involved in smuggling got arrested. They were taken to the so-called Small Fortress: an old prison outside of the city limits that now served as a prison for criminals from the camp and political detainees. Gavrilo Princip, who had murdered the heir to the Austrian throne, Franz Ferdinand, on 28 June 1914 was imprisoned there until he died from tuberculosis in Theresienstadt.[78]

The men imprisoned in the Small Fortress had to carry out extraordinarily taxing physical labor.[79] Barely one in a hundred survived such torments. Women had it easier. They spent a large part of the day trying to free themselves from lice, remained in bed, and slept in order to suffer less from hunger. Only three times during a week would they receive some food: a few thin slices of bread and some watery soup. The local population knew about it and made the sacrifice of secretly leaving some food on their windowsills.

On 23 February 1945, the last group of cigarette smugglers had been brought to the Small Fortress. In the lists of the names sent to our office I found quite a number of crossed out names, with the annotation "to Stapo on 23 February 1945."

Another grave crime consisted in sending illicit letters. Those who got caught were punished the same way as the cigarette smugglers.

Since it was forbidden to express wishes on the postcards one wrote, there was an extraordinary scarcity of certain things. Among the rarest and most coveted objects were toothbrushes, hairpins, soap, elastic bands, thread, and stockings. I exchanged a second toothbrush that I had brought for a large piece of sausage—a precious treasure. The sausage came, of course, from a charity parcel.

Sending parcels to Theresienstadt was permitted.[80] A large percentage of shipped packages did arrive at the camp. Few people in Germany knew about it, since the confirmation notes for these parcels did not always arrive. The Czechs were better off in this respect. They were allowed to have a parcel, up to forty pounds, sent to them once a month. Family members and friends bought what they could, of course, and sent to their imprisoned relatives and friends what they could spare.

Whoever did not receive any parcels went hungry. One of the most important events in camp life was receiving a package. When somebody received a note that a parcel had arrived, they could leave work and hurry right away to the post office. The SS had opened the boxes before, of course, and examined the contents. Sealed tins were always confiscated right away.

The most beautiful parcels were the Danish and Swedish charity gifts. Mrs. Strauss, in whose kitchen I lived, received quite a few of these marvelous packages. She affectionately shared the contents with her roommate and many others. I think that just for this reason I shall always love Danes and Swedes.

The Danish government was watching over the Danish Jews as well as it could. The Danish Jews had been deported by the Germans after the occupation.[81] The Danes received parcels from their country at regular intervals.

Swiss parcels came through the Red Cross in greater numbers. They were standardized packages that generally contained cheese, sugar, sausage, vitamins, and sardines.

We do not know how long the SS held on to such packages before releasing them for distribution. Often it must have been several months. *The last lot of 870 parcels from Sweden were found and distributed after liberation in May 1945. Of the 870 persons for whom they were destined barely 70 were still present. That last consignment of charitable gifts must have been stored for months, for how, in the war chaos of the last months, could such gifts have managed to travel from Sweden across war-torn Germany and on to Czechoslovakia?*

I worked at the central office, where we identified those who were to receive parcels. In April 1945, I saw on the list the name of a long-ago friend from my youth who I learned had died in Theresienstadt in May 1944. Her brother, a conductor in Switzerland, did not know that his sister had died and kept sending his packages. His old mother had died shortly after arriving in the camp. She was nearly blind, and had suffered heavily. She had managed to obtain a Swiss visa after endless interventions by her son. But in the fall of 1942 Hitler's regime no longer let Jews leave Germany, even if they held a visa. So the old lady ended up in Theresienstadt. She died in one of those gigantic barracks, lying on the bare, stark floor. Pauline Meyer was the widow of Richard Meyer, professor of chemistry, who, at the behest of the Kaiser Wilhelm Gesellschaft, had edited the *Gmelinsche [Gmelins] Handbuch für anorganische Chemie*.[82] A reference work without which no chemical laboratory and no scientific research institute could function.

If we had known how terribly people were starving in Theresienstadt we would have sent them bread and potatoes for years. But we did not know. We had no news. In the occasional postcards there was never a request for bread or other food. We did not know that inmates were strictly forbidden to ask for anything. This is the only excuse that we, who lived in Germany, can offer for having let so many of our deported relatives and friends suffer from hunger. In comparison to what inmates

While in Theresienstadt, Eva jotted down on this page from her day calendar the "death dates" (*Todesdaten*) of friends and relatives who had died before her arrival. "18 January 1944, Jobst Hirsch / 16 January 1944, Toni Hirsch / 3 November 1943, Paul Hirsch / May 1944, Else Hirsch to Auschwitz / 5 February 1945, Bianca Israel to Switzerland / October 1944 Julius and Erna Levin on transport / 31 January 1943, Grete Bloch / October 1944, Lotte Pariser." Julius and Erna Levin were likely deported to Auschwitz earlier than Noack-Mosse realized while she was in Theresienstadt; see *Gedenkbuch Berlins der jüdischen Opfer des Nationalsozialismus* (Berlin: Druckhaus Hentrich, 1995), 752, 756. ("Also miscellaneous personal documents including Jewish identity card," p. 6, Wiener Library Document 504d/1) in Theresienstadt received, the rations received by Germans during the war were downright abundant. And yet in reality the German rations were likewise very limited. The rations of bread, potatoes, and sugar were apparently the same in the camp as in Germany. But apart from these basic rations there was nothing else in the camp, whereas in Germany one could freely buy vegetables and countless other items.

We were paid extra for night work. So, for instance, five hours of night work were worth sixty grams of liver sausage. In the first six weeks we received a total of two pieces of meat weighing about seventy grams each. It was cured meat, a gift from the Red Cross.

We got a notion of the dimensions of the reserves when the Russians doubled our rations of bread and potatoes right after the occupation. Once, everybody received sixty grams of cheese. Cheese was such a rarity that I could exchange thirty grams of cheese for six hundred grams of bread.

Thirty grams of cheese for six hundred grams of bread. Two cigarettes for a three-day ration of bread; a piece of lipstick for a four-day ration of bread. An onion for a week's ration of sugar, which was fifty grams; two stems of leek for eighty grams of margarine. The craving for food items that were not distributed was so immense that incredible amounts were paid for minute quantities of food items that were different from what was distributed daily. Trude Zülzer drew portraits for a pound of flour or a pound of marmalade. In earlier days she had sold her pictures to galleries and museums and did portraits of German state secretaries. Based on little photographs, she painted many portraits of people's family members who had been deported to Poland, to the extermination camps. I gave her a jar of marmalade filled with oat flakes for a portrait she made of me.

The price of bread fluctuated according to the ration we received. Sometimes it took days to negotiate the exchange of lipstick for a loaf of bread. The quality of the lipstick had to be taken into account: was it new or old, hard or soft? A piece of lipstick signified more than a blotch of red on the lips. It signified the world outside. It makes no sense to ask how that little piece of red could be so important for a woman who did not know whether the following day she would be taken to Auschwitz to be gassed. It just was that way. *We heard later from women who came from Auschwitz that there, a piece of margarine mixed with shredded red pencil was a substitute for real lipstick.*

Such complicated negotiations, carried out with all due ceremonies, were naturally a lot of fun, too. To jump into a negotiation by specifying what one wanted to exchange—whether a piece of lipstick or anything else—was considered to be in "poor taste," just as it is for the Chinese who have special complex rites for every small transaction.

We also loved to exchange cooking recipes. It was not only simple wartime recipes that were shared. To the contrary: the greatest favorites were the most refined recipes from the days of peace. The greater the hunger, the greater the apparent need to discuss the most extravagant recipes from peace time. The idea of eating just strawberries with just whipped cream was frowned on. Strawberries represented only the basic foundation of dishes that used copious amounts of eggs, whipped cream, maraschino cherries, pistachios, and other glorious goods we had not seen for years. We reveled in recipes of Czech "Torten," which were composed of five different layers. Not a single one could be missing; otherwise, the end product just would not taste right, we were told, especially the Germans, who were unfamiliar with the marvelous Viennese and Czech recipes.

One evening I was sitting in my smoky kitchen with my customary bowl of barley soup. I had cut for myself two slices of black bread to accompany it and was considering whether I could afford to have a third slice without affecting my rationing too much with such extravagance. Just then I heard through the open door Mrs. Strauss' voice, in whose kitchen I was living. "Frau Evchen," she shouted, "I forgot to tell you yesterday the following: for children's feasts I recommend a special dish: Chaudeau buried under a thick layer of whipped cream, but it has to be put into the refrigerator right away."

(I found out later that such conversations about food and recipes were common in all the camps. Men, who could not carry on a conversation about recipes, used to speak about meals they had enjoyed in different good restaurants.)

9 April 1945

Last night I was awakened. I should get dressed fast—a new transport
had arrived—I must help with registration. I went to the so-called
sluice, the transit station, that I had arrived at seven weeks ago as a
newcomer. This time, I was on the other side and beheld the vaulted
chamber, which I had first seen on 22 February as through a fog, as an
"ancient inmate." I recognized the faces of those who were working at
the sluice. Some of them had been working there for years. The man
who collected the money and counted it was familiar with all European
currencies. He was a former banking official from Berlin, a thin, tall
person suffering from tuberculosis. His suit was shabby, the sleeves were
too short and frayed. On this cold April night he wore a thin woolen scarf
wrapped around his neck. He constantly coughed. He continuously
rubbed his hands over a small stove we had lit in a corner of the large,
cold vault. He looked like Bob [Cratchit], the poor scribbler from the
Dickens Christmas story.

On this cold morning, which began at three o'clock, I had the experience of observing the frightened faces of the new arrivals, their timid-
ness, and how everything was arranged in order to increase their fear.
Scared, they all gave their money away and allowed themselves to be
pushed around like defenseless cattle from one station to another.

I was sitting at the first sluice and had to ask the new arrivals their
names and cross them out on a list. It was a transport of 350 Slovaks and
Hungarians. They came from a camp in Hungary. That camp had been
cleared because of the danger of approaching Russians. In spite of the
great haste to empty the camp, however, they had been able to take along
everything that was important: pigs, tools, sewing machines, carpentry
tools, chicken, and cows.

There were two ninety-year-olds among them, a man and a woman.
Since they were too weak to walk, they were transported past us on
stretchers. The old man had folded his hands, his face was calm and
solemn. His papers indicated he was a doctor. He had with him on the
stretcher an old-fashioned umbrella with a bent crutch. It looked as if it
had been a constant, faithful companion to its owner from the time

when he was still walking across the country helping the sick. A child, maybe four years old, passed us. He did not know his name, nor did he seem to have any family members. A young woman began taking care of him.

As is the case among Hungarians, some were blond with blue eyes, while others had black hair and dark, fiery eyes. Seeing these very different types, [Joseph] Goebbels's racial madness seemed more absurd to me than ever.[83] The blonds were northern figures of Siegfried— Goebbels's propaganda could not have imagined anything more perfect; the dark ones were typical southerners. All showed the same kindly and at the same time sad smile when asked for their personal information. They were very helpful when it came to spelling the very difficult names of their hometowns, in which at least five consonants followed one another, which made them hard to write down. They sang the names of their hometowns with the melodic accent of the Hungarians. Many of the women had several children.

10 April 1945

Reports about the war are favorable. Cottbus, Neisse, and Hanover are reported as having been freed. We must, in our offices, continue to pretend to be working for eternity. Two ladies from the Slovak transport, accomplished secretaries formerly employed by the state, are transferred to our office.

All the new arrivals tried, of course, to work in their former professions. But this was possible only for doctors.

Poor hygienic conditions, crowded living spaces, malnutrition, and mental instability offered favorable ground for all kinds of illnesses. The average weight of women was between eighty and ninety pounds, sufficient for survival but not for resisting illnesses.[84] This explains the high percentage of deaths.

What could be done in a community where there were courts but no attorneys, music in the evening but no music lessons for children growing up? There was need beyond doctors and the very few court employees dealing with petty thievery, selling stolen goods, etc.: need for office workers, medical orderlies for the hospitals, craftsmen, street cleaners, firemen, janitors, men and women to work in the kitchens and laundries, women for the German arms industry. Two Christian missionaries living in Theresienstadt who had Jewish ancestors were, for instance, employed by the fire brigade. I found this out while reading through the identity cards.

All the professions were represented. As I found out reading the documents, there were also two beekeepers.[85] Since the SS was fond of honey, these two men continued with their profession. They practiced beekeeping in the gardens owned by the SS, so when they were standing by the beehives, and the windows of the premises were open, they could catch snatches of German and English news services. *They did so until the day on which the SS disappeared for good, and the flag of the Red Cross started to flutter on the church tower: a sign of humanity and of active love for your neighbor.*

One could move freely only within the limits of the city, and there, only in the part allowed for Jews. The SS men and their families lived in the other districts where Jews were not allowed to enter.

Jews also worked in establishments outside the city: at the laundry, the mill, in the fields. They went to work every morning, watched over by the gendarmerie. In one establishment all kinds of objects were fabricated for Germans who had suffered bomb damage: all manner of arts and crafts like bags, saucers, etc. The two arms-producing factories as well as the arts and crafts manufacture received orders and the necessary materials for production. These were the only establishments creating a surplus and doing productive work by normal economic standards. The rest of the ghetto subsisted on the funds that had been taken away from the Jews. As for offices, laundries, bakeries, hospitals, the court, shelters for the countless sick and elderly, children's homes, none of these carried out work with a view toward a future life.

The registration offices were filled with hundreds of people working on complicated certificates of repair, coupons for food, etc., completely unproductive work. For the most senseless reasons one was wakened at night in order to produce meaningless index cards or lists for the SS. The only advantage of such superfluous work: extra hours were paid with food products. But since working during the night made one hungrier, the small amounts of additional sausage or bread would be eaten up right away. All was superfluous, and one was never full in Theresienstadt.

The working day lasted ten hours. There were no free days, neither Sundays nor feast days, nor Easter or Christmas, nor any Jewish feast days. A free Sunday afternoon was introduced only in 1944. On such free Sunday afternoons people washed, aired the beds, tried to get rid of bedbugs, mended socks, and whatever else they needed to do to preserve their possessions and to remain clean and free of lice.

Since every establishment had different hours, and in the armament factories there was also a night shift, there was continuous coming-and-going in the rooms, continuous heating of meals on the tiny iron stoves, and hence, constant unrest and noise.

The Jews had carried out productive work when, having been thrown into terribly insufficient housing and unhygienic conditions, they started to construct baths, to install water pipes and electric conduits, and tried to improve sanitary conditions. They created carpentry workshops in order to produce bed frames, tables, chairs, and shelves. They installed laundries, shoemaker and joiner workshops, hospitals, and infirmaries. They carried out Robinson Crusoe–like work under the most difficult conditions. They created in exile, under the most primitive conditions, what a person needs in order to live and to die.

Little by little, the SS offered the Jews old furniture and objects taken from the confiscated Jewish apartments. They of course first took for themselves what was good and useful. They left behind poor quality, old-fashioned, impractical furniture items.

In the kitchen where I lived, there was a so-called shelf for cans and cooking pots. I could not wait for the moment I could burn this monstrosity. *When I found out that I only had a few weeks left in the camp and that only some technical complications delayed my exit, I burned, with great satisfaction, some of the most grotesque caricatures of furniture. I did not want anyone else to end up with such monsters in their kitchen.*

Theresienstadt was called a "top-quality ghetto" in SS jargon. From the outside all had to look irreproachable. The SS insisted on having the lists in the office typed on perfect paper. In spite of the great scarcity of paper during the war all had to be registered on the best quality sheets and in many colors. Since the wishes of the SS outweighed those of any other authority in the Reich, there were, for example, quantities of wood available that had not been seen for many years in the Reich because of war conditions.

There were all kinds of writing paper, from rough Dutch laid paper to the finest Japanese paper, carbon paper of all colors and qualities, thousands of filing cards of different colors. And all this for no other purpose than making lists of people who were meant to be exterminated at a time prescribed by the SS.

Still in January 1945, when there was not even a splinter of wood to be found in Germany for repairing a roof badly damaged by bombing, the SS brought in wood for the construction of a new bowling alley. The SS liked to bowl. Also plans for expanding the ghetto had been completed. Later on, mixed-race people belonging to the Christian community were to be deported to Theresienstadt, as well as anybody who had even a drop of Jewish blood.

As I have already mentioned, once a month everybody received a small amount of paper money valid in the camp, on which there was a picture of Moses with the Tables of the Law. I, for instance, received fifty kronen per month. With that, I could go to take a bath for two kronen each time. I could drink a cup of substitute coffee in the so-called coffeehouse. That also cost two kronen. This coffee was accompanied by two lumps of sugar. The so-called coffeehouse, which held about a hundred people, was always overcrowded because of the two lumps of sugar. It opened in the afternoon. Admission cards for entering it were distributed. Little old men and women who did not have to work anymore frequented it with pleasure of course—it was a kind of sitting room and a place to warm up.

Apart from that, one could, about once a month, buy some spices, like mustard, home-grown tea, and other little things with one's ration card. These cost around twenty kronen. If one was lucky one received, about once every six months, some thread for sewing or mending socks, tooth-cleaning powder, and other little things. But since the number of ration points was limited one could never purchase all that one needed.

A 100 kronen note from Theresienstadt. (courtesy of United States Holocaust Memorial Museum Collection, Gift of Hana Rehakova, Accession No. 1992.132.21)

Relatives outside of the country who believed it was possible to send money to Theresienstadt sometimes sent large sums. These foreign transfers were confiscated of course. The receiving person only received a receipt that was worthless. We heard of cases where the SS had directly demanded that family members pay large amounts for their relatives living in Theresienstadt so that they could be transferred to a nice old people's home, where they would receive good care. Like everything else, this was just a lie. In the years 1942–43 people continued to sleep on bare floors. If they were lucky they received, months later, the right to use part of a mattress. Since later on there were continuous transports to extermination more space could be found for a lone individual on the existing furniture. At the time when Theresienstadt housed sixty thousand people at once it must have been hell.

11 April 1945

Everybody receives two hundred grams of rice, a donation by the Swiss Red Cross. What is happening? Restlessness increases.

12 April 1945

There is a sensation at the office in the morning. The head of the Jews, the clever Eastern Jew with a rough face, rushes excitedly into our office. We should draw up a list of all the Danish Jews as quickly as possible. We run to the piles of cards and lists. After an hour we found out that this happened by the order of a gentleman who had arrived by car a few hours earlier. Feverishly, we put together lists of the four hundred Danes.[86] And around three o'clock in the afternoon the news spread like a fire through the city: the Danes will leave immediately. The same evening, they flocked together with their belongings in the sluice, where up to then no person had entered in order to leave the camp, apart from the transport which had left for Switzerland in February 1945.[87]

The meter-high placards enumerating punishments and threats for not declaring and handing over valuable objects were taken off the walls of the sluice. A foreigner was to come to get the Danes. It would have made a bad impression if the foreigner had seen these signs. For the four hundred persons who were to leave and were to stay in the sluice until their departure, the carpenters fabricated wooden beds in haste—yet another trick intended to ensure that the foreigner would see how neat the Jews' beds were in the camp.

Those who were departing radiated happiness. They received a short laconic notice: "You are destined to be part of a group going out of the country."

Nobody knew whether the trip would take them to Sweden or to Switzerland: the only peaceful oases in Europe in the spring of 1945. Those who were departing gave their friends whatever they had saved and reserved. They did not take along anything edible since they were to receive food—the miracle continued—from the Red Cross. Cars were to come to pick up the Danes. We are waiting until late at night, but the cars do not arrive. Upset, we go to sleep.

13 April 1945

The cars still have not arrived.[88] Would they be able to go across the front lines? We were in the middle of a war, after all. Two young girls, brides of two Danes, used the delay to obtain permits to go along. The head of the Jews had hastily performed the marriage ceremony for the two lucky couples. No one knew—nor did they care—whether or not this marriage rite would be recognized abroad. The important thing was, for those taking part and also for those who were not part of it— but we were all more or less part of it with our hearts—that they could leave the camp. Waiting, waiting, waiting the entire day. Where have the cars been stopped?

14 April 1945

In the late afternoon the cars finally arrived, large white cars with a red cross on them.[89] At the border of the city the SS asks the Swedish drivers to get out of the cars: no foreign driver is allowed to enter the camp. The Swedes did not even answer; they did not pay attention to the SS men, who were nothing to the drivers. They did not get out of their cars but instead just crossed into the limits of the city. Later on the SS invited the Swedes to use the bathroom in their house and to eat with them. The Swedes sent their officer with the reply that they had brought their own food with them, and would spend the night in their cars.

15 April 1945

A stupendous spring day, impossible to forget. Birches swinging in their first tender green; the sky a soft blue, the air mild and already warmed up by the sun. Four hundred happy persons, surrounded by us all, get into the beautiful cars. The Swedish drivers distribute chocolate to those surrounding them—real chocolate. For the first time in four years the SS stands by, silent in the background. A long line of cars is forming. In front, three motorcycles, then a long row of passenger cars, the kitchen vehicle, an ambulance. The gates of the city are opened, the trip begins via war-torn Germany toward a peaceful, free country.

It was like a miracle. All perceived it that way. Some old persons who had been locked in Theresienstadt for four years considered the departure one of the most moving experiences of their entire life. It was as if the loving God had come down from heaven and lifted up a whole heap of poor animals with his own arms.

In the afternoon of that same day the Danes left [led by Johannes Holm]—protected by the Red Cross and under the flag of humanity, making their way through a destroyed and bleeding land in its last convulsions—there was a terrible setback.[90] Two hours after the departure of the Danes a new transport arrival was announced. We could not believe our ears when the announcement came. Was this possible? More victims driven toward us still? We were deeply depressed. Two closed animal transport train cars arrived. They remained unopened for several hours on the rails of the sluice. The SS had installed rails all the way into the city center in order to handle the transport of people more swiftly. It was toward midday; the SS men had their noon break. They had no intention of shortening that break, so the two wagons, already on their way for days, had to remain standing in the sun for another few hours until the order to open them came. One hundred Hungarians and Slovaks came from a camp in Austria—another transport directed to us because of the approaching Russians. Again, I sat at the registration table writing down the names of the newly arrived.

16 April 1945

More whispering. It is said that another new commission is coming. The restlessness increases. Nobody knows for sure what is being negotiated. Rumors swirl around. Is the SS going to withdraw? Are they packing? Workers from the tailor shops say that complete outfits for a hundred men are being prepared. A field kitchen is prepared with a carriage attached to it—a trailer furnished in Bavarian rustic style, all brand-new. Since every one of us had acquaintances in each plant, it was impossible to keep these preparations secret, even if the SS had ordered to keep them "top secret." Twenty-two thousand kilograms of medicine and pharmaceuticals, given to the Jews by the Red Cross, were packed away for the SS. There was such haste to establish the lists that in the office, we could not take time off for lunch. I myself proof-read those lists. In their greed, the SS men ordered anything good and useful in the camp to be packed. Ultimately, the SS could not possibly take everything away because it was too late. The Russians were approaching. So much had to be unpacked again and left in the camp.

News on the radio reports the ever-tightening encircling of Czechoslovakia. Where could the SS go now? The SS ordered us to hand in all rucksacks. Who was to receive them? There were rumors that it was for the Germans who had to flee from Prague. Nobody knew anything more specific. I decided right away not to give up my rucksack, that true companion on many trips, but rather to hide it. I dismantled it into two parts. The frame went into the box with dirty clothes, the sack itself under my bed. These were not very original hiding places, but there were no others. To my surprise I found another rucksack already there. Trude Zülzer, my roommate, had also decided not to give up the rucksack with which she had unsuccessfully tried to flee across the green border into Switzerland. She thought the spot under my bed was particularly good. A little while after that, an acquaintance who slept in a room with many others came to visit me. She did not want to give up her rucksack at the last minute either. Since she slept in a room with many people she did not dare to hang on to it. Since I lived by myself in my room, nobody could control me, she said. I lent her my little suitcase into which she could put all that was in her rucksack, and then she brought me her rucksack, the third one in my kitchen. This one I hid in the coal box. For days I would come across these rucksacks when looking for something else. It was almost like hunting for Easter eggs. A few days later it was announced that there were enough rucksacks delivered to the SS. They needed only five thousand, and that number had been reached. I was so glad not to have fallen prey to that silly ploy.

17 April 1945

All rumors and conversations deal just with one thing: when will the SS men, their wives, and children leave? According to one rumor, the last members of the SS left the preceding night. But a little later a call comes from the Oberscharführer [Siegfried Seidl] who was supposed to have already left Theresienstadt.[91] It is depressing. One has to be patient. It cannot go on for much longer.

18 April 1945

The high point of psychosis, which is spreading like an illness. The uncertainty drives everyone mad. Around 1:30 in the morning excited people were marching through the streets, since a rumor about liberation had spread through the city like wildfire. Nobody inquired who the liberators were, nor where they were. Processions formed and marched through the streets singing. They sang and made noise until sensible individuals summoned the elders of the community to calm the masses and implore them to return to their houses immediately. For it was strictly forbidden to be on the street after 10:00 in the evening. The excitable crowd calmed down surprisingly quickly. The encouragement of those who were thoughtful and responsible helped. Before the SS arrived the greater part of the crowd were again in their own houses. The Jewish elder had to march through the town with his hands high and a machine gun pressed to his back, but no shots were fired.

19 April 1945

New rumors. A transport of many thousands of people would be brought in during the next few days. We could only shake our heads. Where could new people come from at this point? Czechoslovakia was already encircled. One could still expect some eight to ten thousand people, it was said. We studied the few small maps that we kept hidden and tried once more to understand the current war situation. Alas, our news was often imperfect!

20 April 1945

They are really coming. The excitement is so great—I haven't experienced anything like it in the camp before. The first seventeen hundred persons enter the city on foot. They are creeping, barely able to move. They are not people, just creatures on two legs, wrapped in rags.

21 April 1945

They are rushing in, rushing in through all gates, all streets. It is impossible to create index cards for all the new arrivals, who would normally be immediately registered. Thousands of new arrivals. In great haste, makeshift mass lodgings are established in vacated barracks. It is there that the poor new arrivals are sent. Roughly seven thousand have arrived thus far. All were wearing blue-and-white-striped uniforms: a sign that they had come out of concentration camps. Some of them had to walk hundreds of kilometers. There were no more train connections. They had had to march on open roads supervised by the SS. Those who fell and could not continue were shot or beaten to death. Some had spent weeks crammed together in tight wagons; a piece of raw rutabaga was the only food they had for a day. There were also raw potatoes in their wagons. The sick and the dead were thrown on them while en route. One could not cook because of the lack of fire. The dead contaminated the potatoes. Half decomposed, those potatoes were dumped out at Theresienstadt, the crowds fell on them and dragged them to their homes. After all, potatoes were very spoiled and scarce in the camp at this time of the year. The dead and those who could not walk were dumped into trucks, sacks over their heads. If they were still alive, their bodies twitched. The skulls had lost all flesh and shrunk to the size of children's skulls. They were pure bones with skin covering them; the color of the skin was a greenish yellow. They arrived so hungry that we gave them little bits of bread and sugar. But then they were fighting for that, and we had to forego this well-intentioned but impossible act of charity. The new arrivals were given double rations right away. But at the beginning their stomachs could not take in practically anything, least of all the constant brown barley or potato soup. Thousands contracted intestine infections after a few days. They were not people anymore; they had become wild animals. Even these were once made in God's image, whispered many of us on the streets.

These new arrivals had to be partially closed in behind barbed wire, because they represented a danger for the rest of the camp. They were given clothes, and the rags that were on their bodies were burnt in order to prevent epidemics. The fires burned for days. The clothes were sources of infections of all kinds. But there were not enough clothes in the wardrobes to dress the thousands of nude people. And more and more of them were arriving. They were coming from different camps in Germany and Austria.

22 April 1945

More and more arrivals. I see a train coming through the streets, a long train of elderly people and children. They walk very slowly; they barely manage to put one foot in front of the other. They have traveled all the way to Theresienstadt in cattle cars. An old man is carrying an office chair as his only piece of luggage, on which he probably sat during weeks of travel. Silently, the procession drags through the streets. We remain standing by the houses. The odor of people who have not been able to wash themselves for weeks reaches us. We, the inhabitants of Theresienstadt, suddenly realize that in the last weeks we have lived practically in luxury compared to these people.

The camp administration no longer knows how to house the unending stream of people. How to clothe them, how to disinfect them, how to keep infection out of the camp? The sanitation authorities work like mad, the doctors never remove their coats. They go through the barracks and the camps, and wherever there is still among the sick or dying the slightest sign of life they do all they can in order to keep their severely reduced bodies alive. Some of the doctors got infected during this selfless work; they contracted typhus and died a few days before the final liberation.

They came from some twenty different camps from all over Germany and Austria. At that time, we heard for the first time the names of the camps: Ohrdruf in Thuringia, Flossenburg, Oederan, Ravensbrück, Krems, Kaufering. We got more information about Bergen-Belsen and the immense camps in Saxony, in Czechoslovakia, and Lower Austria. And as the trains of misery pass through the camp, an announcement is fastened to the black boards. Here it is word by word:

Notification by the Jewish Self-Administration Theresienstadt
No. 68

22 April 1945

Mr. [Paul] Dunant, a commission member of the International Red Cross, who visited the Jewish settlement in Theresienstadt on 6 April, arrived here again yesterday, 21 April 1945, and issued a declaration at the meeting of the elders.[92]

This declaration affirms that the Jewish settlement of Theresienstadt will continue to be supported by International Red Cross in every respect. Effective immediately, Mr. Dunant will handle all questions regarding help for Theresienstadt.

This declaration is made to the inhabitants of the Jewish settlement of Theresienstadt with the firm expectation that everyone will be aware of their responsibility for the community and contribute to ensuring the continuation and success of the ongoing work and to preserving peace and order.

This communication, so dry and curt (because there still were officially some SS members in Theresienstadt), saved the lives of nearly thirty thousand people.

The incredible has happened. Theresienstadt and its inhabitants are now under the protection of the ICRC [International Committee of the Red Cross]; in other words, they are saved. But we in the camp never found out why and how this had happened. *How was it possible that there still were some, admittedly very few, SS members in the camp, and at the same time Dunant together with the Jewish elders were publicly announcing that we were under the protection of the International Red*

Cross? Later it was rumored that one of the SS members had betrayed to the Red Cross the plans to have us all murdered, but this has never been confirmed. (H. G. Adler has presented in detail the complex negotiations between the SS and the Red Cross in his book about Theresienstadt.)[93]

A person often reacts to certain things very differently from what he or she expected. Instead of dancing with joy and thanking God for being finally saved—according to every human expectation—everybody simply took in this notice very calmly. Only our brains registered it. Our minds, our feelings, were too shaken by the arrival of the twelve thousand pitiful figures that had just come in to permit us any happy feelings. Among the newly arrived people from the concentration camps some of us had discovered friends or relatives who had left Theresienstadt a year or more ago. But most people spent days looking in vain for their husbands, sons, daughters, and friends among those who had just arrived. They were roaming through the barracks, where the new arrivals were lying on the floor, since there were not enough mattresses on hand. Like dogs, they followed the smallest tracks.

24 April 1945

The number of newly arrived is now estimated at twelve thousand. The camp population before this influx was seventeen thousand. Within one week it had increased by 70 percent. Emergency kitchens were installed, voluntary help sought, all the baths closed to the general population, since the newly arrived had to be thoroughly cleaned and disinfected. This was the greatest preoccupation. It became evident right away. Not only typhus, but all imaginable diseases in existence had been brought in. Many of the newly arrived could not be saved in spite of the doctors' self-sacrifice. They died of exhaustion. The daily lists of deaths contained many "unidentified" entries. Nobody knew their names. Since they had been put into concentration camps none of them had any documents on them. Only a number was tattooed on their arm. Where in the world today is the mother or fiancée still crying for these nameless people? We buried them in our camp shortly before the liberation.

25 April 1945

As we hear, from so far away, that two-thirds of Berlin has already been occupied by the Allies we begin our fight against contagious diseases and death. The registrar—who is also the person taking care of the burials, is a former bank employee from Vienna, and like many Viennese has the famous "golden heart" of the city—comes to our office to give a report every day. His duty is to look in the barracks for the dead and take care of their removal. What he needs most at the present time are hospital orderlies. He searches for them and offers them the most desired thing at present—a special supplement of sausage. But he cannot find enough. There are not enough rubber coats and gloves to protect the orderlies from getting infected. His stories are gruesome but often have also an irresistible comic element, as when he describes, with his Austrian accent and impressive gestures, without leaving out the smallest detail, his fight against lice and dirt. In his capacity as undertaker, he must accompany each dead body to the crematory, situated outside of the ghetto. Nobody is admitted there. Only he is allowed. And he describes to us those walks behind the hearses with the corpses, tells us what the outside world is like, whom he meets, the spring outside the camp, the fields, the starlings, the young lambs in the pastures, and the lilacs that are at the point of blossoming. His stories are sentimental, comic, and sad at the same time. And in the middle of his long reports he interrupts himself and complains about not having enough help to carry the dead bodies and about how the typhus cases are increasing. We should pay attention lest in the end we too are infected by lice.

29 April 1945

Appeals on the blackboards about how one can best protect oneself from lice, which spread typhus. Since the warmer season is approaching and one does not have to wear any thick woolen clothes anymore, and since, according to experience, during the warm season the epidemic dies out, we have hope that it will not spread further. The most important thing is to make sure that the lice cannot hop from one body to the other. That means we must avoid contact with other people as much as possible.

Since there were specialists for everything in the camp, there was, of course, one also for lice, an elderly university professor who shared his expertise in lice in a singing voice. But what he advised remained theoretical because there simply was not enough room to isolate the sick. And the new arrivals did not stick to quarantine prescriptions. They had had enough of being behind barbed wire fences and did not want to repeat the experience. This was understandable but did not help the fight against infection.

30 April 1945

Mussolini has died.[94] In the camp, the danger of typhus is growing. Some SS people are still here. Pessimists do not believe that the end of the war is imminent. Perhaps the tepid weather contributes to the depression.

2 May 1945

The news of Hitler's death is officially announced.[95] The SS lowers the swastika flag at their headquarters to half mast. It is grotesque, almost unbelievable: the Nazi flag at half staff to mourn Hitler's death in the ghetto of Theresienstadt. We all went by the town hall on that day. Everybody had to see it with their own eyes. Even the most convinced pessimists begin to dream on this day and make plans for the future. Martha Mosse, my friend and companion, and I unfortunately do not have anything else but coffee substitute to drink on this day. We drink a cup together, symbolically, and sit together by the window of her poor little room. The view opens onto a wide landscape with mountains in the distant background. The great distance seems to us not so great on this day; we close the distance with our thoughts.

On this day, the man who oversaw the production of the family indexes, which was so neat and complete but had to be destroyed at the last moment, lit his first cigarette in forty months. He had saved it for this moment. It was a historic moment when he lit his cigarette and said, "I have been waiting for Hitler's death for forty months, forty months for this moment. If we, those who spent these months together, had known before that our life here would last for forty months, many of us could not have endured it and would have taken our own lives. It is good that we did not know that after the invasion the war would last another year. Too many have been sacrificed. We cannot therefore express our joy loudly. We know what a miracle it is that we, a little remainder, are still alive today."

4 May 1945

Our work days are reduced from ten to eight hours: for us, the first direct consequence of Hitler's death. We still see some people in SS uniforms. From hour to hour the news about armistice is expected. One last air raid siren. The cordon around the city is already, imperceptibly, loosened. Some "Aryan" husbands suddenly appear in search of their deported wives. They are being hidden, and immediately a Jewish star is affixed to them so they won't attract attention. The Czech gendarmes become approachable.

The Small Fortress—the old prison of the city—is opened; those who have survived file past us in long rows, most of them women, freshly washed, poorly dressed, but all remarkably clean. Among the men, very few have come out of this prison alive. There are political prisoners among them, who have sat in this jail for many years for the smallest infringements. Also some Jews from our camp are among them. Hundreds march by us. Harrowing scenes play out during this march. Some recognize friends and family. They break out in loud crying. This is something that I experienced again and again in the following days, weeks, months: when two people found each other, both cried. Nobody could laugh.

Mr. Dunant is back. Wherever his white car with the red cross on it appears, a crowd quickly forms. He is slender, tall, and tender. He has light, semi-closed eyes and blond hair combed to the back. We all know now his light-gray, checkered, well-tailored suit. When he first entered the Jewish city, he was unarmed and hatless. We see him often now un-armed and hatless as well. He is, for us, more than just a single person—he embodies the living idea of love of thy neighbor, and in my recollection our freedom will always be tied to this slender man with light eyes, not coming on a donkey with an olive-tree branch in his hand but in a white car with a red cross painted on it.

5 May 1945

Suddenly, we see women with high heels and modern hats on the streets. We knew right away: the first "outside" wives from Czechoslovakia had arrived. For out on the street, no woman from the camp wore anything on her head besides a scarf. Each one of us had arrived with a hat, and later, on the way back home, many of these unmodern hats suddenly resurfaced.

Today, still no official news regarding the unconditional surrender.

6 May 1945

The last SS man has disappeared. Finally, it is real. The last pessimists begin to breathe freely. Mr. Dunant and his office occupy the abandoned SS headquarters on the town hall square. The white tag with the red cross is affixed also on this door. On the church steeple, too, a banner with the cross flutters. An official announcement is issued: the International Red Cross protects us and return transports will begin as soon as possible after the end of war.

Here is the text of the pronouncement word by word:

To the men and women of Theresienstadt!

The International Committee of the Red Cross has taken over the protection of Theresienstadt. The representative of this commission, Mr. Dunant, is in charge of administering Theresienstadt. He has entrusted the undersigned members of the former Council of Elders with the direction of self-administration.

You are safe in Theresienstadt! The war has not ended yet. Whoever leaves Theresienstadt will be exposed to all the dangers of war.

Theresienstadt has taken over the care of the martyrs of the Small Fortress. This demands increased work productivity, which is also necessary for preparing the transports back. Work has to go on. Whoever refuses to work will be denied return transport.

Mail written in any language is no longer censored or otherwise restricted. To facilitate the sending of mail, every inhabitant who so desires will receive a stamped postcard as soon as they are available in sufficient quantities.

Newspapers will be obtained and publicly displayed.

Severe illnesses that still prevail here at this time make it necessary to impose certain quarantine rules. They must be meticulously observed.

When the war ends, return transports will begin as soon as possible and in accordance with the prescriptions of the government.

Maintain peace and order! Help us in our work, which should make a transport home possible. Everybody should stay in place to take care of the work assigned to them.

Dr. Leo Baeck, Dr. Alfred Meissner,
Dr. Hermann Klang, Dr. Eduard Meyers[96]

Theresienstadt, 6 May 1945

The first Czech national flags appear in windows. Had the war really, definitely ended? Like everybody else in the world, we also were feverishly awaiting the final notice of unconditional surrender. At one stroke we were no longer officially cut off from the world.

7 May 1945

Everybody has received a small bar of chocolate, proper chocolate.

From one hour to the next we await the arrival of the Allied troops, who are apparently near Lobositz, which means very near. At the office, the lists of the twelve thousand new arrivals wait to be written.

Then, in the evening, the time has come. Mr. Dunant announces in German and French the unconditional surrender from the balcony of the town hall. We listen to the news silently.

In order to celebrate this Martha and I cook the rice given us by the Red Cross.

The Czechs tear off the placards written in German. They are replaced by placards in Czech. This is patriotic but impractical, since among the twenty-seven nationalities represented in Theresienstadt each knows some German, but no one understands a word of Czech, except the Czechs and Slovaks. The following day, placards in German and Czech are affixed.

Another fifteen hundred people arrive tonight, prisoners of the concentration camp at Oranienburg near Berlin. They had been on their way here for four weeks. It had taken twenty-eight days to cover the distance of three hundred kilometers. Sixty-seven of them were on the brink of dying, including a black man.

8 May 1945

A divine May morning. I take an early-morning stroll through the empty streets. The sky is a most tender blue. The Red Cross flag fluttering on the church tower stands out against the blue sky. I pass by the former guard headquarters. Nobody prevents me from entering the town hall.

A few hours later wild arms fire begins around the city. So, the first shots we hear come after the ceasefire was announced. Until then no bomb had fallen, no hand grenade had been thrown into the city. Now, the last rearguard fights of the retreating Germans against the approaching Russians began.[97] We hear the heavy artillery from afar. A hand grenade was tossed into town, two people were lost.[98] We are warned not to go near the fortification walls or to leave the city. In town, cases of typhus are increasing; we are declared a quarantined zone.

In the evening, the first Russians march past. They do not enter the city; they march along the so-called Aryan road, a road that directly borders the camp. We had often stood behind the tightly constructed wooden fences, peering through knotholes to try and catch a glimpse of outside life. We could see some trucks or other types of cars that were passing by. Quickly, candles are brought and mounted on the wooden fences. They radiate a festive glimmer in the warm May night. Entire planks are torn from the fences so we can have a better view of the soldiers.

The endless march of the Russian army begins: tanks with the awkward movement of antediluvian animals, wagons whose shape has not changed in three thousand years, laden with baggage. From passenger cars, narrow-faced yellow-skinned tartars greeted us with a lazy yet elegant hand wave; Cossacks on the little Panje horses pass by, glued to their horses as if they were just one being. They sit on the cannons. They are often blond and blue eyed like the north Germans; they throw us some cigarettes and bread. Different types of Russian peasants march by, with their high Slavic cheek bones, a good-natured grin on their broad faces, playing the harmonica and singing. There are also Russian women soldiers, almost all big boned and with coarse faces. They all pass by. A high-ranking officer pays a courtesy visit to the city administration, which has now returned to Czech control.

9 May 1945

For twenty-four hours we have a troop of English prisoners here. They are now being sent to their troop divisions. The first Allied soldiers. We stare in astonishment at the high-quality cloth of their uniforms. We adorn them with lilac, which is just starting to bloom. We talk with them. We try to explain to them where they are. It is not easy to make them understand that we are prisoners only because we are Jews and not because we have committed some crime. The English soldiers had been working for two years on a nearby farm.

In the evening, we are standing by the fence so that we can see the never-ending march of the Russians again, and a pale SS prisoner is led past us. He has his arms raised. People hoot at him and insult him. I am a little sick at this sight. To read about the fear of death written on a man's face does not mean much in most cases. But to see it oneself, to see the fear, to hear the shrill whistles and celebrating shouts, to feel hate fluttering around oneself, is something quite different.

At night the Dutch arrange a religious service of thanksgiving and sing the first song celebrating the liberation.

10 May 1945

Little by little the Russian occupation is established here. They replace Mr. Dunant, whose task has been completed. Every single person takes their leave of him and says goodbye and thanks him in their thoughts. The first placards in Russian appear. There is a search for interpreters.

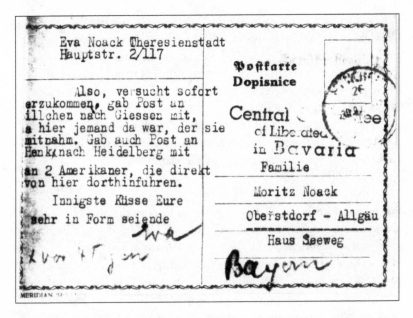

One of the postcards Eva sent back home after the war ended. She wrote it on 5 June and it arrived on 25 September 1945: "So, trying to get here as soon as possible. Gave stamped post to Billchen headed to Giessen who was here. I also gave mail for Henk to two Americans heading directly to Heidelberg from here. / Deepest kisses to you, I am well, and remain yours, Eva." ("Also miscellaneous personal documents including Jewish identity card," p. 7, Wiener Library Document 504d/1)

We write the first postcards and give them to the first car drivers going to Prague. None of us has known until this time that there is no railway service in Germany, no means of transportation or possibility of traveling, and that this will be the case for many more months. We faithfully and bravely use every means of sending mail by post, *but out of the twenty-five postcards that I wrote to Oberstdorf only two arrived, quite a while after I myself had returned home in good health.*

11 May 1945

There are always new groups of Russians passing by. Many of them throw us some bread and cigarettes and also sausage and chocolate.

Their first German prisoners come into the camp to work. They can be recognized by the red swastika painted on their backs. Their main task is to carry away the dead bodies and clean up debris in order to prevent epidemics.[99] The first cases of intestinal typhoid fever are appearing.

14 May 1945

The first American comes to our office, naturally a soldier. He is looking for his deported parents. He obtained furlough from his division stationed somewhere in Germany in order to search for them here. But he did not find them. His large brown eyes acquired a melancholic expression when the lady at the information desk could only very briefly say that "they were not on the lists." It must have been terrible to stand here after all those years, as he did, still hoping to see them again, and hear us respond with a few barren words: they were not in our files. We could not even tell him whether they had died a natural death or been sent on a transport to the East. All documents had been destroyed. In spite of the terrible news this young American was incredibly patient in answering all the questions that we put to him. Besides the plain fact that war was over we did not know anything else yet. Little by little we heard more about the extent of the destruction in Germany.

The Russian *Kommandant* [Major M. A. Kusmin] was small and had an elegant appearance.[100] He begins to work and at such pace that those accompanying him, those who worked with him—interpreters, specialists of all kinds—can hardly keep up with him. He is practically running through all the sections in order to get a complete overview of everything. He runs into my friend and me in the evening, when we are marching across the courtyard of the barracks with our little soup pots, and he asks us, with the aid of an interpreter, what we hold in our hands. We answer: "Our supper." He asks again: "And nothing else?" We answer: "Nothing till tomorrow morning." "And what do you get in the morning?"—"Coffee."—"That means, water," he adds right away.

14 May 1945

Those who carry the dead bodies receive new overalls. With their white suits, to which hoods have been added, they look like the good

Samaritans in the Middle Ages at the time when the plague was ravaging
Florence. But one thing we do notice right away: Russian sanitary divisions work fast and thoroughly. More and more exhausted people from
the concentration camps are dying of pneumonia, heart failure, dysentery, and other previously unknown fever illnesses.

In great haste several large barracks are being emptied in order to
receive the sick. From now on—a new Russian method—the sick, in
spite of high fever, were put right away into disinfecting baths in order
to kill the lice, so that even the sick would not be contagious. Their
hair, of course, was cut off. This soon turned out to be an efficacious
procedure, although often a very strenuous and weakening one for weak
patients with high fever. Men and women, old and young, were hastily
put together in the same rooms. There was not enough care-taking personnel on hand in order to treat all the sick appropriately. Fortunately,
most of the cases were not dangerous. Mortality rates among women
barely reached 6 percent; among men, it was three times higher, that is,
18 percent. Women proved once more to be much more resistant than
men.[101]

15 May 1945

Starting today the food rations have increased. The reserves are so great
that we can receive a pound of bread daily. The rations of potatoes,
sugar, and fat have been increased as well. We are told that we should
receive a ration equal to that of a Russian soldier. But for the time being
some of these numbers are only ink on paper, since transport conditions
are too complicated, and fresh meat is especially difficult to acquire. But
already a few days later we receive such quantities of bread that we can
save them for the people who are traveling to Germany. For some time,
we received only barley. But it was well cooked, sometimes mixed with
sugar and at other times with peas coming from German troop reserves,
appearing suddenly, at times even with some meat. We always had
enough to satisfy our hunger.

The Russian *Kommandant* assembles the inhabitants and reminds
us how serious the danger of typhus really is. Everybody must do what
he can in order to prevent spreading the epidemic. A fourteen-day

quarantine is imposed on the city. Afterward, all will be done in order to dismantle the camp as quickly as possible. The *Kommandant* is an admirable speaker. Although I do not understand a single word of Russian, I always knew more or less what he was talking about, even before the interpreter started to translate into German. He accompanied his words, pronounced in a melodic sequence, with slight movements of his hands. And he had perfect facial expressions. He had something of a fatherly quality, although he was rather young. At the second assembly I could tell from his movements how much he felt like the responsible father of us all, admonishing us to behave well and to be reasonable, diligent, and reliable to the end.

The relaxation had been too good; as a consequence, the desire to work in the camp after all these years was practically zero. But there were still a number of important tasks before us, which had to be dealt with: fighting the various epidemics and breaking down the camp, with all that this involved.

The camp was constituted at that time of some thirty thousand persons. The original body of seventeen thousand persons had to do all the work, since the twelve thousand ill and emaciated concentration camp inmates were too weak for real work. In spite of the expected discharges, a number of establishments—the kitchen, the hospital, some repair workshops, the offices responsible for completing paperwork—had to function smoothly until the very last moment. It was imperative to establish lists as accurate as possible of the twelve thousand new arrivals. These lists would later provide an important foundation for the search centers. None of the twelve thousand newly arrived had personal identification papers. We were all convinced that not all of them had furnished correct information about themselves. Since young people who had not yet reached eighteen years of age received additional rations of food, all men who believed that they did not look much older than eighteen indicated that they were not yet eighteen years old.

16 May 1945

The first reporter from British Radio appears in our office: Mr. [David] Graham of the BBC.[102] The mutual questioning begins. He spoke excellent German. He wanted to know a lot about us. We, isolated from everything, wanted to hear even more. With endless patience he answered all questions, which we wildly poured out standing around him. His soft brown eyes looked at us searchingly. Ready to help, he picked up mail that we desired to post. He wanted to be back in London within five days. *A short letter to a sister living in London [Hilde Mosse] thus arrived very soon. She forwarded the news to friends and relatives in America. And so it happened that my poor husband was the last one to hear about my fortunate escape, although Oberstdorf in Allgäu, our residence at that time, was only some 400 kilometers away from Theresienstadt. Oh, if only he had already known then that I was already smoking American cigarettes and had received the first charitable donations from America.*

18 May 1945

A pair of swallows built a nest on top of a lamp in the open promenade around my barracks, in front of the constantly dark kitchen in which I live. The construction was finished within a few hours. The lamp sways, but this does not disturb the birds. Thousands of swallows regularly take up residence in the old barracks. The noise produced by people and the constant running in the overcrowded corridors does not disturb the birds. They return every year, messengers from another world. My pair of swallows seems to be especially animated. They twitter without interruption. Especially just before the light of dawn, around three o'clock, they carry on vivid conversations and wake me from my slumber. I get up and go to the open windows in the corridor. The entire enormous building is full of the twitter of the numerous swallows. The air is filled with their singing and the clapping of their wings. The old ruins live.

19 May 1945

Today, the first Berlin inhabitant appeared. He had come by bike covering a distance of some 250 kilometers in ten days. He is visiting his fiancée and finds that the atmosphere here is very peaceful. The meals are so plentiful that he decides not to go away again for the moment.

Klaus Mann, the son of Thomas Mann, comes into our office in the capacity of American soldier and reporter for different American newspapers.[103] From his south German accent and his especially cultivated German, I immediately recognized him as a native German from an educated family. After a few questions I know with whom I am speaking. What follows is an intensive back and forth conversation. In a few minutes I see the world before me and hear about many of our mutual friends in America. He did not get to see his aunt Mimi [Maria Kanová], the first wife of Heinrich Mann: she had already traveled to Prague.

20 May 1945

Work in our office increases with every day, with every hour. Daily, more and more Allied soldiers arrive, asking about their and their friends' relatives and acquaintances. But since only 7 percent of those deported to Theresienstadt were still alive, we rarely were able to give good news. However, once I could tell a young Czech, who was looking for six deported relatives, that five of them had gone to Switzerland in February. After both of us had overcome this delightful shock he asked me timidly, "And how can I repay you for this?"

For days and weeks our main task now has consisted of answering inquiries. Little by little, mail and telegraph began to work again. Telegrams from all over the world were arriving; the whole world seemed to be dispatching telegrams: "Dear mother, how are you? Give us a sign of life; we think of you with love, and will arrange for you to come at the earliest opportunity." And how few were the opportunities to wire back a positive reply. Thirty-five thousand dead, ninety thousand deported to Poland: such was the sad outcome after four years. Answering the inquiries was an unsettling occupation. Each telegram caused a large group of relatives either endless joy or endless sorrow. We kept searching through the lists and archival entries. And the entire office staff felt happy each time we rediscovered somebody alive and could pass on the good news. To share laughter and tears with others remained one of the most beautiful qualities of ghetto dwellers. They had not lost the art of sharing joy or compassion.

The number of those who have died since 20 April has climbed to 1,089. In the evening I listen to the English radio broadcast for the first time in months. My neighbor, a Czech architect, received a radio as a gift from a Russian on the road who had picked it up as war booty somewhere. The Russian had probably grown tired of carrying the heavy appliance. So he gave it away to the first person he met. It was a feast to hear for the first time again the four well-known knocks of the broadcast.[104]

21 May 1945

The Czechs who do not have to go far to get to their hometowns are starting to leave the camp. Their friends pick them up in cars, transports are being organized, and some of them simply walk away. They leave their baggage with friends; it will be fetched later. The administration looks for volunteers who will work until the camp is broken down. They offer a good salary to take care of all the final work to close the camp. The Russian commander announces that there are currently two thousand sick people in the camp area, two-thirds of them sick with typhus.

On the streets, unattended horses run around. No one takes care of them. They were left behind somewhere during the moment of the hasty retreat by the Germans. They seek food and water.

22 May 1945

Martha, as a "long-time camp resident," receives one of the magnificent charity parcels today that are slowly being distributed from the immense reserves of the Red Cross. These are gifts that arrived at the camp after the original recipients were already dead or had been deported. On the magnificent Swedish crackers, we put Swedish butter, sausage, marmalade, and cheese; add to that tea from the American parcels, sweetened with sugar and milk. After this meal we both have the feeling that it is unimaginable for either of us that we might ever have to suffer from hunger again.

23 May 1945

I was wrong. I am hungry again. *In my diary it says, "The more one eats, the greater the hunger."*

Lists, more lists, new ill persons, new dead ones, new entries in the mortality indexes. The corpse transporters now receive so much sausage that they are very zealous at their work, and there are no more dead bodies lying around. The German prisoners also help. Little by little, some order returns to the mass of people. Everybody knows by now that all will be done as fast as possible to allow them to return to their homeland as soon as possible. Exact plans have been elaborated and have established the basic scheme for camp departures. At least in theory. In practice it looks somewhat different. In spite of the quarantine, so-called "wild departures" are increasing. The impatience to get out of the camp is growing and is making people nervous. We are repeatedly told that the roads are in no way really safe yet, that bandits are roaming around everywhere and that therefore we should wait until regular, secured transports are available. Many do not listen to the warnings and prefer to leave even if it takes weeks to march home. They do not have the nerve to wait any longer and leave in small troops.

24 May 1945

In these and the following days not much new is happening. We never stop writing lists: according to nationalities, according to hometowns. Forms are distributed to be filled out: where one wishes to be transported; whether one still has any family members at home. One of the great worries is the many old people who are totally alone and have nobody. Often, all their family members had been deported to Auschwitz, and it is not yet possible to find out whether there still may be some relatives living somewhere in the world. Where should these lonely old people go?

26 May 1945

I have taken on myself to establish lists of the surviving Berliners. In the next few days, two deputies will try to get through to Berlin in order to negotiate a return transport with the Jewish community there. *One hundred and twenty-three transports with some fifteen thousand people in all went from Berlin to Theresienstadt. Out of the fifteen thousand some fifteen hundred survived the deportation. Among those who were not returning, half were elderly people who died rather soon after their arrival,*

and the other half was sent on the eastern transports and the so-called workers'
transports to the Reich, a dreadful machinery of death (see preface).

The organization of return transports is slowly gathering steam. It is
difficult to imagine the technical difficulties that have to be overcome,
since neither the mail nor the telegraph function anywhere in Germany.
Only couriers are available, as in the days when there were no railways.
The town of Jena, in Central Germany, is the first community that has
a bus for transporting its citizens back home. Other towns followed
soon. Step by step, the marvelous reality reached us. The barracks
courtyard suddenly filled with cars sent from German cities, driven by
chauffeurs who spoke all the dialects. And then, these same cars were
filled with people who were going home. It takes us a good while to get
used to such miracles.

2 June 1945

An American from the Red Cross comes with a comrade who is looking
for his parents. I take the two gentlemen around, since one of them
does not understand a word of German. I realize how moved he is by
what he sees. He does not say a single word, only groans silently from
time to time, and his young eyes look frightened and helpless. I show
him the rooms in which people were living one on the other for years. I
tell him—like all the others—that some time ago all traces of people
who were not alive any longer had to be destroyed. Even the X-ray
plates were driven away by trucks back then.

Taking leave, he puts into my hand, among other things, a few issues
of the periodical *Life*. This was the moment in which I really started to
feel alive again, since I am a journalist. The whole world is with me
again. I keep reading until late at night in my smoky kitchen; next to
me is a bag of dried plums, a charitable gift from the Americans. I do
not know what I enjoyed more: the taste of the sweet dried fruit or the
first pictures of the wide world. It was a magnificent evening.

5 June 1945

Eighteen hundred dead, among them four hundred dead from typhus
since 20 April 1945. Today, they announced the end of quarantine.

Again, the Russian commander assembles the camp inhabitants and talks to us in a fatherly way: now that the danger of typhus has passed, we have to maintain utter cleanliness and remove all rubbish and waste. If not, we would get a typhoid epidemic next. *(The report of the Dutch Dr. [Aron] Vedder, "Typhus and the Means to Fight against It," Amsterdam, 1946, explains that the author lived in Theresienstadt since 6 September 1944 and describes the epidemic. According to Vedder, twenty-five hundred were infected by typhus; five hundred died as a result.)*[105] This comprises only proven cases: some sixteen hundred people arrived in Theresienstadt already nearly dead, and expired before a diagnosis could be established. Hundreds of them were probably infected by typhus. Statistics of 9 June 1945: 447 dead, among them ten doctors.[106]

Departures, many departures.

Seventy-five Czech nurses and sixty doctors arrive by plane from London. They had heard about camp conditions on the radio. They arrived fresh, unspent, and ready to help and to support our completely overworked personnel. Medicine also arrived from Switzerland by plane.

———

There is not much to be told about the following days, which became weeks, until finally on 1 July 1945 the car from Augsburg arrived and picked me up. I was in the camp long enough to see the young swallows born on my promenade lamp post, their little heads at first covered with shaggy gray tufts that then turned smooth little by little. All five of them sat at the edge of their nest. Cheeky, full of curiosity, and twittering, they looked down at the freed Jews and undertook their first flights.

I was in the camp long enough to see German Nazi women, who had been taken prisoners, cleaning our primitive toilets, mostly with slightly pinched lips and a nasty look in their eyes. The Russians did not give them very much to eat, but their good-natured Jewish supervisor gave them some bread whenever she could. She thought, just as I did, that the mere fact of being a prisoner was bad enough and that one should not drive one's fellow human beings mad by letting them deliberately suffer from hunger. For hunger does make one mad; hunger does not permit any thoughts other than this: how can I get enough to eat? Once there is enough to eat, one can start thinking of other things with a clear head and no more greed. It was only when I managed to have enough bread and had satisfied my excessive hunger that I became a normal person again and could think of the many things that occupy a normal person's head. But as long as one is hungry, one is just an animal, an obtuse or violent animal, melancholy or docile, depending on one's disposition, temperament, and education.

After the quarantine ended, I received a passport and could go for evening walks in the beautiful rich surroundings outside the little town as much as I wished. I roamed through the fields; the crops were green around the stalk, the rhubarb ready to be picked. But nobody picked it, since the German population that had lived in that region had been expelled. I crossed wide fields in which young peas were starting to mature. The fields were abandoned; there was nobody taking care of the harvest. I picked lots of small delicate pods and ate the tender green husks that contained tiny peas. I pulled out small onions and felt their biting flavor on my tongue. I roamed through empty orchards with not a soul in them — in a few weeks they had returned to a state of wilderness, because there was no one to take care of them.

The grounds of the Jewish farm were resplendent in their vigorous green. The lettuce, planted for the SS, was already getting very tall. A year before, a Jew caught eating fresh vegetables without permission was sent to Auschwitz. Now, there was practically nobody there to reap what had ripened.

Until the day of my departure, 2 July 1945, I answered telegrams without interruption at the office. The number that arrived increased every day. All contained inquiries about relatives that were missing.

At my departure, I left a great heap of unanswered telegrams on my desk. I felt guilty about leaving the office forever.

Then I packed my belongings. We left with a bright sun and a blue sky. At the city gate, I saw the same Czech policeman who in the past months had stood next to me at the office of the new arrivals, pushing the tired and frightened people over to me. We waved to each other smiling. The trip home across a summer land began.

There were twenty people in the car. An old countess sat in front of me for the whole trip. She had spent her two years at Theresienstadt as a totally blind person. She had arrived with a thick, completely white braid around her head. It had been cut off right away, like the hair of all other arrivals. By now, two years later, a new, thick white braid had grown. It was an even braid that covered her head, and I stared at it during the whole trip.

I had got over being separated from my comrades at Theresienstadt who had different destinations. Martha Mosse wanted, of course, to get back to Berlin, where her constant, loyal friend Erna Stock, with whom she had lived, was anxiously waiting for her.[107] She had spent two years in Theresienstadt at this point. Silent, loyal, with tears in their eyes they stood by the car as I was departing. They themselves did not know whether they would find any kind of home at the end of their journey. Their belongings had been scattered in all directions; their thoughts had no fixed point they could call home.

The fog that had formed an impenetrable wall between my home and me dissipated a little more as the car was leaving the camp.

As we were driving across gray, provincial Pilsen, an American soldier was standing at the market place, regulating the traffic. He was the first American soldier whom I saw as a policeman. He had an orange in his hand, and while he had to direct the traffic, he was playing, throwing the golden ball into the air with his left and catching it with the right one. He was obviously having a lot of fun. So was I, watching. *Since that day I have seen a good number of American soldiers working as policemen. Not all were playing with oranges while they were on duty. But almost all of them look as if they could at any moment. I thought of the Prussian traffic regulators, and even the thought that one of them could be playing with an orange while on duty amused me again and again.*

We drove through Prague, which was mostly undamaged, and our eyes wandered everywhere, seeing many, many people, tramways, some destroyed houses. Shops, partly closed. But in the bakeries that were open there was much bread displayed in the windows, which was a re-assuring view.

At nightfall we were not allowed to keep driving. In July 1945 nonmilitary vehicles could not drive at night. We had reached the Czech-Bavarian frontier. We were directed to a totally empty house where we could rest until the next morning. There was only a little straw on the floor. All the rest had been taken away by the owners. Several young American soldiers showed us to our night camp and expressed regret that we would not have anything more comfortable. But it was totally unimportant to us, of course, whether we would have something a bit softer or harder to lie on during this last night.

At the end, a very young soldier went through the rooms once more and asked us whether everything was "all right." I said: "Yes; the only thing that is lacking for complete comfort would at best be a cup of tea or coffee." The young man knelt in the dark and asked where we were coming from and what had happened to us. And while we smoked a cigarette together, just two little glimmering points glowing in the dark room, I told him in English about our experiences of the last months, with a very low voice, in order not to disturb the others. From time to time the young man directed his flashlight toward me in order to look at me. My story seemed inconceivable to him: that a woman should have been separated from her husband by force and that we all would have died miserably if the Allied troops had not freed us. Maybe he understood at that moment why he had gone to war.

The cigarette had gone out. He got up quietly, whispered a soft, almost tender-sounding "good night," and left on tiptoe.

Thus ended the first day of my new life. I slept marvelously, wrapped in my blanket and my coat. Nature has given me the ability to sleep well anywhere. Even during the trip to the camp, when we did not know where we were being taken, I slept well. My companions only shook their heads. "Just in case, as a reserve," I told them.

We resumed the drive the next morning, through sleepy villages, across provisionally erected concrete bridges, through more or less bombed cities. Conversations among us were not very animated. Everyone was occupied by his own thoughts, very far away from those who surrounded him.

Those among us who had already spent several years in the camp saw for the first time the destruction of the war.

As we arrived in Augsburg, things came full circle for me. The friend in whose house I had spent the night on my way to Theresienstadt was expecting me. I slept there again. This woman received me as a mother would a child she had believed lost but that had finally returned, a woman I had seen twice in my entire life so far. She, her friends and acquaintances, as well as many unknown people, were glad, in a heart-warming, intimate way to see us return.

Travel conditions at that time made it impossible to think of proceeding to Oberstdorf at any point during the next four days. I could not get in touch with my husband by phone, since telephone communications were restricted to the occupying forces. My husband knew that I would come home soon. Several messengers had been sent to tell him that I was in good health and that a car would go to Theresienstadt in order to fetch the deported people.

I decided not to get impatient in those last days either. First, I went to the hairdresser in order to have him correct my hair, bleached by soda water. At the hairdresser's I could enjoy the luxury of civilization: soap, warm water, hot hair dryer, and clean towels "on the house" for me because I was returning from the concentration camp. The other customers had to bring soap and a clean towel themselves. Then I went into various stores, content and aware of my freedom, and purchased with great pleasure a poor-quality lipstick, powder for the face, and all kinds of other little objects. It felt wonderful to be able to go a store and pay for what I bought with real money.

In these days I came to know a young student from Munich who, having participated in the Hans and Sophie Scholl resistance, had been sent to prison and also had been freed by the Allies.[108] We came to an understanding right away regarding the ever-present bugs in every camp. We recognized one another as bedbug experts, to the astonishment of those who heard this conversation. It is possible to speak about bugs for hours if one has ever been in a camp. In such cases, one is not concerned about those who may be present. An unending topic, always new. In amazing ways it can connect two persons who do not know each other at all. Yes, "bedbug friendships" are established very quickly and informally.

These days of waiting passed and came to an end as well. Everybody was so kind to me that I would have appeared ungrateful if I had showed impatience to leave. On the fourth day, an old, rickety, gray car without windows stood in front of the door; it could only be a so-called paddy wagon—a car for transportation of prisoners that the army had converted into a hospital car. The journey began. It went on for hours, the car going one way and the other, taking home one deported person after the other, plus many other people who did not want to miss this opportunity to go home. In these days, French occupation forces took over from the Americans. The French, almost all of them Moroccans, wore very clean multicolored uniforms, red fezzes, and multicolored jackets. They looked like oversized toys against the background of green Bavarian meadows and peasants' houses.

One after the other, people were taken home. Then my turn came. During the last leg of the trip I sat next to the driver in order to indicate the way for him. As we were entering the village I saw an acquaintance. He was so stunned that his mouth literally remained open. When I was brought to our house it was exactly 5:00. I heard the church bell ring the hour. It was 7 July 1945. I rang the bell persistently and violently. After barely two seconds the head of my husband appeared at the opened window on the second floor. I only thought, "How many wrinkles, how shriveled, how twisted all the lines on his face, how old he has become. I will have a lot of work on my hands." Then, fast as lightning, he ran downstairs and into my arms. After two more seconds, both daughters came running down the stairs, both looking healthy, fresh, and well.

For the past three weeks they had waited daily, watching every minute and second for my arrival. In those days there was no mail, no telegraph, and no telephone in Germany. They had only gotten a message three weeks prior that I would come home. Since that moment they had been cleaning the rooms, washing, ironing and baking, and even placing fresh flowers into the rooms. The flowers withered and had to be replaced, which was easy because the meadows bloomed. The cake dried, too, and had to be eaten. They baked a new one, and that was not easy because food provisions ran low—even though, before the

Allies arrived, grocery stores had distributed rich provisions, especially butter and cheese. They had just baked a fifth buttercream torte. It was ready in the cupboard.

After my husband had overcome the first shock of our reunion he looked at me thoroughly and started to laugh. He had before him his wife in an old-fashioned gray suit with a jacket that did not fit, in a felt hat, dressed in the clothes of her dead friends. She looked like a school-teacher from the most remote village in East Prussia.

And already the doorbell was ringing. In a blue-white polka dot dress, Amalie Zuckmayer stood in the doorway. Like nearly every day she had taken a small walk from the "Villa Homeland," where she had lived with her nearly blind husband ever since their home in Mainz had been destroyed by firebombing. She came by to find out if my husband had any news from me. My husband had brought the Zuckmayers from Mainz to Oberstdorf. Many years before, she and I had attended the most beautiful premieres of her son, the poet Carl Zuckmayer—including the brilliant premier of "The Captain of Köpenick" at Max Reinhardt's Deutsches Theater in Berlin.[109] She could not believe that I was home. She always looked at people with love. But when she looked at me this day her love radiated not only from her eyes. After a short time, she left so she could tell her husband that I had come home safely.

I went through the house and looked at our possessions. I had not thought about them once during the past months. I went into the closet, and looked at all of clothes hanging there enticingly, freshly washed and ironed by daughters and girlfriends. Then I looked at my two beautiful pearls, the black and the white, given to me by my mother when I was born. Glittering and delicate they were encased in her light blue velvet pouch. Within a few minutes a festive coffee table was set. The fifth buttercream torte was set on the table.

And then there was my beautiful bed with fresh linen covers waiting for me. After twelve hours I had gotten used to civilization again, so much that not having had in Theresienstadt a napkin nor missed it, the next morning I asked my daughter who was setting the breakfast table, "You have not forgotten my napkin, have you?" All was there again, and yet somehow new.

And if later in my life, things ever go badly, and I feel miserable, I will remember this homecoming, but I also will remember the love at my departure, which ensured that I never felt totally abandoned but rather as though I was enveloped in a warm coat.

I also will remember the hours on the train, surrounded by wailing women, not knowing that we would be deported to the ghetto. I will remember the naked people whose hair was cut off to the root, the beds full of bugs, and walls from which all the whitewash had fallen off. I will remember the concentration camp inhabitants streaming into the camp and their heads so emaciated that they looked like the heads of children. And I will remember the people who saw this and, in spite of having spent years locked up in Theresienstadt, were going through the streets in tears, murmuring, "They all are images of God."

I am not afraid any longer. What should I be afraid of? I do not hate people; I have received too much kindness from them. This is not the moment nor the place to speak of the people and the institutions who wanted to send us to die. I am indifferent to those who are halfhearted, of which there are so many. I despise those who do not feel guilty. I have become sensitive, very sensitive, to people, and separate the true from the untrustworthy. My intuition has developed, and my ability to discern has become finer. I believe my sympathy for the poor and the unfortunate is as great as it ever was. But I have become more stringent in what I count as misfortune. Little inconveniences or a lack of comfort do not represent a misfortune for me anymore or anything that could be described by this word. It is not worthwhile to cry over most of the things one loses. But there are certain things that one should never cease to cry about losing. And one should never allow one's conscience to go to sleep. When there is injustice, when evil occurs nearby, do not close your eyes. And in order to help ensure that what has happened will never happen again I have written about what I have seen and experienced.

Eva Noack-Mosse

Appendix 1

Correspondence between Eva Noack-Mosse and George L. Mosse

München 27
Adalbert-Stifter-Str. 81
Telefon 48 10 48

15 August 1952

Dear George,

I respond immediately to your letter which arrived yesterday; if not, one takes too long to answer. The reason: my husband left yesterday, with our daughter, for Zuoz in Oberengadin, where we have a house; he and I have just returned from Berlin, where we visited Martha Mosse (Albert's daughter) and her friend. They live in the large block on Cicerostraße, constructed by Mendelssohn: on Mosse real estate. Now, the whole neighborhood is in uproar—I could not say whether rightly or wrongly—I do not know all the facts—about the fact that you receive "nothing," but the trustee alone is earning a lot. All this could be just empty talk—I have no idea. But I wanted to let you know, so that you might take appropriate measures if necessary. The "people" of the neighborhood think it is somehow unjust that no Mosse can get the money due him. We have of course our own lawyer, but yet for some time we have had to go to Berlin every four months in order to move our case forward. There are not many good lawyers who know how to handle matters of restitution. And they are terribly overloaded, so while they do things right, it takes them a very long time. In addition to our excellent lawyer, we three siblings also have an "agent" who knows the ways and proceeds further with the matters to which the lawyer is unable to attend.

Apart from that, the Olschkis were in Switzerland for quite a while—part of the time with us—they want to try to spend the winter in Rome. The next time I write them, I'll send them your letter. Their permanent address: Olschki, Casella postale 295, Florence, Italy.

It is good that you take care of *The Questionnaire*.[1] Unfortunately, although the book is partially very well written, the attitude of the author is so absolutely lacking in character, so sleazy and nihilistic, that one can only spit in front of him. But he does give a graphic picture of the time and circumstance of the [Walther] Rathenau assassination—even if, naturally, [Hermann] Ehrhardt's [1881–1971] personality has been chemically cleansed. Those people were at any rate the gravediggers of the Republic. But the description of the "salon" at the Rowohlts' is charming, even if—exactly as the entire book—full of such enormous indiscretion that the author deserves a box on the ear just for that. I read it while I was suffering from an influenza, and my recovery was quite a bit delayed because of it.

We were together with the Olschkis when [Douglas] MacArthur gave his speech.[2] Leonardo made comparisons between antiquity (Caesar and Pompeii) and today. The official American institutions are now inclined in favor of [Adlai] Stevenson.[3] By the way, I should like to bring to your attention an article about the Germans by Konrad Heiden in *Life*. Printed in the international edition of 30 June 1952. We do not hear much from Beller, nor do we see him. He is often with a friend of ours, who is interested in his research. He is apparently very diligent, travels much and swiftly in order to see as much as possible of Europe, and has an enchanting friend, a Miss Rochelle, who has also visited us. He was very briefly in New York, for a lawsuit that brought him a lot of money. I forgot what it was about; apparently a lucky coincidence, an accident, or something of the kind. A sort of menacing jackpot . . .

Well, dear friend, it was very nice of you to give a sign of life. By the way, I am planning to come to the US through the State Department next year, on an exchange program or something similar.

Cordial greetings from your
Eva

At any rate, greetings from Moritz and all of us

Munich

5 October 1954

Dear George,

Many thanks for your very friendly letter of 7 September.

At the same time, I am sending to you a printed piece, a copy of the *Frankfurter Hefte*. I have given a copy of the report about Theresienstadt to an acquaintance. When he returns it, I shall happily send it to you, and you may keep it for yourself and your future work. I know very well that such a report ought to be printed, but you know these paralyzed and forgetful ducks here in Germany. Who would want to spend money on publishing a concentration camp report, even if it contains statistical material? But this report, too, will one day be printed in some kind of source collection, where it will occupy the place it deserves.

We just were together with the Olschkis in Venice. As you may know, Leonardo has given several lectures on the occasion of Marco Polo's seven hundredth anniversary in a really wonderful and dignified setting. It was a great success for him. Olschki's address until mid-December is: Pensione La Residenza, 22 via Emilia, Rome.

Leonardo wants in any case to be at Berkeley again by early January next year, since he definitely wants to continue his work on his Marco Polo book. Käthe and Leonardo were in excellent condition. Leonardo worked the whole morning while Moritz, Käthe, and I strolled through Venice. Partly together with Hilde Himmelweit, the indescribably beautiful and engaging daughter of Friedel and Feo Littauer, both of whom were certainly very nice and solid but not kissed by the muses. Please keep this commentary to yourself; otherwise it will get circulated back to me by some relative next year.

I have written a lot of silly things in the last months. As soon as something nicer gets published you will certainly receive a copy. But I can't imagine that you would be interested in the nonsense that I fabricate for women's pages. Since it simply has to be done, I am enclosing a copy of an article from a provincial journal that appeared here many times and apparently was enjoyed by the readers.

Kindest regards from Moritz and me.

Yours
Eva

Eva Noack née Mosse, and Moritz Noack
München 81
Rümelinstraße 12
tel. 98 10 48

10 August 1973

Herrn Prof. George L. Mosse
Pension Joseph Hof
Trivastr. 11
München 19

Dear Georgie,

What a strange comedy of misunderstandings:

Käte Olschki wrote me a number of weeks ago that you would be here in Munich for three weeks in August. And gave me your address here. Carola had told her everything.

A little later she wrote you would be here from the sixteenth to the twenty-sixth.

When I just called the Pension Joseph Hof I was told, to my great disappointment and astonishment, that you had been there for roughly fourteen days in July and that you might return there in mid-August.

Maybe you have tried to phone us but could not reach us.

Moritz and I would very much have loved to see you—once again after so many years.

Now our situation is as follows:

I do want to express myself very clearly.

From August 13 to 20, we ourselves will be in Oberstdorf—a health resort in Allgäu. I was ill for a very long time, shingles with many complications, among other things, neuritis. For the time being I suffer from cough and should go—doctor's advice—to the mountains for a short time, for a change of climate.

But at present a charming young lady, kind of a niece of us all, is in Munich. Vivianne Hirsch, great-granddaughter of Leonore Cohn, née Mosse, granddaughter of Paul Hirsch and Else Hirsch, née Cohn, daughter of Günther and Wally Hirsch. Günther is Bianca Israel's nephew, so it's all very simple by Mosse standards. Can you follow?

She is working for a large public relations firm: Herrioneth & Partner, phone number 29 37 45, all day long. The office is situated right at Max Weber Platz, Maximilianstr. 45.

Be so kind as to call her—telephone messages are being transmitted. And make some kind of appointment with her.

She has a mission. In my name. Since I do not know whether Moritz and I will see you. I definitely hope so.

You must certainly remember that I gave you my diary—many, many years ago, a little after we got reacquainted in 1951 (?) after your lecture at the Amerikahaus: my diary from Theresienstadt. If my memory is right you found it extremely important as a source for materials—and also well written; since it is factual, I do not spread rumors but put down my own experiences and observations.

Only parts of it have been published so far: in *Frankfurter Hefte* and *Die Welt* several times on different occasions. Carl Zuckmayer and Walther von Hollander, respected authors—to name only two—found it excellent. So I have the idea that it might be possible for you to transmit it, with a recommendation that it be be printed, to the Leo Baeck Institute in New York. I can hardly imagine that a recommendation from a historian and specialist of your standing would not persuade the people there that they ought to publish this diary.

The copy that I sent you 1001 years ago, which was typed on very poor-quality paper, might be somewhere in your house or library. I had the manuscript copied again. No changes—only some documents have been added, which I did not use at that time but that are present in my archives.

Just a final side remark: Our *Bundespräsident* [Gustav] Heinemann [1899–1976] and his wife Hilda [1896–1979] intervene, as you certainly know, steadily and repeatedly in favor of the oppressed minorities and those that have suffered harm. So they were at the wreath laying ceremony for the murdered Jews in Holland. We saw it on television. After that I wrote a letter to Mrs. Heinemann, in the name of so many who cannot do it anymore and enclosed money from Theresienstadt, which at that time was issued only there and had to be "earned"—the so-called Moses money. And what did she do? She appeared at our house without announcing herself—in order to give thanks. A little later I sent her the newly typed diary. She was grateful and moved.

This letter has become lengthy—but I had to be more specific this time.

I hope that we shall still see you in Munich. As soon as we come back I shall call you at Joseph Hof.

I also hope that you and Vivianne Hirsch will get together in the meantime.

With the most cordial wishes, of course also from Moritz.

Yours,
Eva Noack—née Mosse

Eva Noack-Mosse

13 October 1973

Please read this letter first [before the August 10 letter that precedes this one]

Dear Georgie,

The letter written to you on August 10 this year was sent to me only now, upon request, by the very nice and trustworthy owner of Hotel

Joseph Hof, since we were away from Munich twice more, for shorter periods of time, and it had to be forwarded to me reliably.

So, at the end, nothing came of a meeting here in Munich.

Now I would, of course, gladly send you my Theresienstadt diary. The premises are the same as a few months ago, but I will not do it before I definitely know that this is what you want.

Therefore, I cordially ask you to briefly write me and let me know.

The fact is that today, in the *Time* magazine dated October 15, I read your name with reference to Mr. Kreisky—what a nice coincidence.[4]

In the meantime, I have recovered—up to three quarters—from the shingles and all its various consequences; hopefully, the rest will follow some time, although all the experts agree in saying that it may take years. But my head is healthy.

For today, the most heartfelt wishes, also from Moritz.

Yours,
as ever,
Eva Noack

8 Munich
Rümelinstraße 12

31 October 1973

Dear George,

Many thanks for your letter of October 23. How nice that you will be coming to Munich again sometime soon.

We shall certainly be here all winter long, and are looking forward to seeing you. Special thanks for your advice regarding the Leo Baeck Institute. I shall write Mr. [Fred] Grubel today and use your name. Thanks to later additions from my notes the new version is definitely better—even if Zuckmayer and Hollander already liked it very much back then. I won't bring you any shame with this manuscript. By the way, I am not disinclined to contribute perhaps a small grant. The whole matter is too important for me—even if it is not more than one more voice in the chorus of much documentation—yet important for posterity, in my opinion.

We are all well again—thank God, even if both Moritz and I must still take special care of ourselves. But my head is o.k.

Munich has really become very pretty, and one can live well here: plenty of Prussians, and loud Berliners cause *almost* no offense now.

Very cordial greetings from both of us.

Always yours
Eva N.M.

Munich

26 July 1976

Dear George,

Today I would like to send you, with most heartfelt greetings, the photocopy of an article of mine, which appeared not long ago in Zurich's daily *Die Tat*. It will surely be of interest to you to hear that after its appearance, the editors received many articles that depicted little events in the "Third Reich."

When are you coming back to Munich?

We are well. Moritz celebrated his eightieth birthday last month! One can't believe it (uses a typical expression by Clown Grock: im-po-po-possible) [*nit für m-ö-ö-glich halten*].

Last summer we again visited Käte Olschki in Berkeley, we had a wonderful time traveling through the redwood forests.

We hope that you, as a historian survived well the two hundredth anniversary [of the United States Declaration of Independence]. We already did not know where to go—and then all that stuff you had to go through.

Most cordial wishes from my husband and myself. We hope you will survive the elections in November well. That Jim Carter . . . One loses the appetite to eat peanut butter . . .

Cordially yours
Eva Noack-Mosse

Eva Noack-Mosse
Rümelinstr. 12
D-8000 München 81

12 December 1976

Dear Georgie,

In mid-July 1977 Ullstein Verlag in Berlin will celebrate its one hundredth anniversary. (By the way, on this occasion, a festschrift will be published, which will include an article I have written about the monthly magazine *UHU*).

The state museums, Preussischer Kulturbesitz (long title), have decided to organize a huge exhibit on this occasion, which will present a snapshot of the Berlin press landscape at that time.

Mosse Verlag plays, of course, a great role in that. I am heartily collaborating with a Dr. Andreas Grote, since I am the only person whom Dr. Grote can consult.

I have already sent them a genealogical tree, unfortunately not quite complete, and must ask for your help.

1) Dr. Grote would like to know when and where your father, Hans Lachmann-Mosse, died in California.

2) When and where your mother, Felicia Mosse, died.

3) If possible, they would, of course, also want to exhibit the original portrait of Rudolf Mosse painted by Franz Lembach, 1898. Under the picture it is written: "In possession of the heirs of Rudolf Mosse." I found this indication in a book: "Zeitungsstadt Berlin. Menschen und Mächte in der Geschichte der deutschen Presse" by Peter de Mendelssohn. Im Verlag Ullstein (1959).

Dr. Grote would also like to know whether Dora Panofsky is still alive. Would you by any chance know? My understanding is that she already died many years before Erwin Panofsky died.

May I use this occasion to send you best wishes for Christmas, also on my husband's behalf, and wish you all the best for the New Year.

Most heartfelt wishes
Your
Eva N.M.

University of Wisconsin
Madison, Wisconsin 53706

Department of History
3211 Humanities Building
455 North Park Street

Dear Eva,

Many thanks for your letter.

1. Hans Lachmann-Mosse died in 1944 in Happy Valley, Lafayette, California.

2. Felicia Mosse died in February 1972.

3. The matter of the Lembach painting is more complicated. I asked that it be sent to me. That was some time ago and through a certain Mr. Terart in the Mosse Stift. But if it has not been sent yet, it could be lent, of course with an appropriate insurance, and then be sent to me after the exhibition. The picture is kept in the basement of the Stift—unless it is already on its way to Madison.

As far as I know, Dora Panofsky died quite long ago: Panofsky married again before his own death.

I am at your disposal, with pleasure. The Mosse archive at the Leo Baeck Institute in New York could also have something valuable (archivist Dr. Milton).

I'll certainly pass through Munich sometime this spring, since I shall not be teaching this year and will spend most of my time in Europe. Hopefully you will not be in Berkeley at that time.

All the best,
George

16 May 1984

Dear Werner and at any rate Georgie,

I thank you both, at any rate, for the separate copy of the article about the life and work of Albert Mosse. What a life, and what different ways his reputation went.

I was sorry, dear Werner, that we got to speak only once. But even so we found out quite a bit about each other.

Once more, heartfelt thanks from your "second cousin"—which is really only half true.

Always yours
Eva Noack

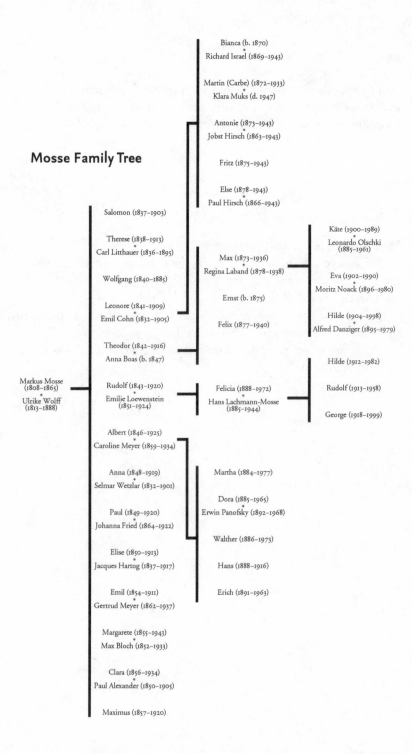

Mosse Family Tree

Bianca (b. 1870)
*
Richard Israel (1869–1943)

Martin (Carbe) (1872–1933)
*
Klara Muks (d. 1947)

Antonie (1873–1943)
*
Jobst Hirsch (1863–1943)

Fritz (1875–1943)

Else (1878–1943)
*
Paul Hirsch (1866–1943)

Salomon (1837–1903)

Therese (1838–1913)
*
Carl Litthauer (1836–1895)

Max (1873–1936)
*
Regina Laband (1878–1938)

Wolfgang (1840–1885)

Leonore (1841–1909)
*
Emil Cohn (1832–1905)

Ernst (b. 1875)

Felix (1877–1940)

Käte (1900–1989)
*
Leonardo Olschki
(1885–1961)

Eva (1902–1990)
*
Moritz Noack (1896–1980)

Hilde (1904–1998)
*
Alfred Danziger (1895–1979)

Theodor (1842–1916)
*
Anna Boas (b. 1847)

Markus Mosse
(1808–1865)
*
Ulrike Wolff
(1813–1888)

Rudolf (1843–1920)
*
Emilie Loewenstein
(1851–1924)

Felicia (1888–1972)
*
Hans Lachmann-Mosse
(1885–1944)

Hilde (1912–1982)

Rudolf (1913–1958)

George (1918–1999)

Albert (1846–1925)
*
Caroline Meyer (1859–1934)

Anna (1848–1919)
*
Selmar Wetzlar (1832–1901)

Martha (1884–1977)

Dora (1885–1965)
*
Erwin Panofsky (1892–1968)

Paul (1849–1920)
*
Johanna Fried (1864–1922)

Walther (1886–1973)

Elise (1850–1913)
*
Jacques Hartog (1837–1917)

Hans (1888–1916)

Emil (1854–1911)
*
Gertrud Meyer (1862–1937)

Erich (1891–1963)

Margarete (1855–1943)
*
Max Bloch (1852–1933)

Clara (1856–1934)
*
Paul Alexander (1850–1905)

Maximus (1857–1920)

Appendix 2

Glossary of Names

Baeck, Leo (1873–1956). Before the Second World War, Dr. Baeck was a national leader of the German Jewish community, a role he continued to play after arriving in Theresienstadt in 1943. In the camp, Baeck gave lectures and helped coordinate the community. Philipp Manes remembered Baeck as the most popular public speaker in the ghetto and was thrilled to have him speak on the occasion of the five hundredth lecture Manes oversaw.[1] Eva mentions Baeck as one of the internationally renowned Jews who were sent to Theresienstadt. The Mosse family papers are housed in New York at the Leo Baeck Institute, the research center founded in Baeck's honor.

Bergel, Karl (b. 1902). Born in Dortmund, Bergel was SS-Untersturmführer, camp inspector, and deputy to Obersturmführer Dr. Seidl. Bergel worked as a hairdresser before the war. In Theresienstadt he was known for being drunk and breaking the ribs and skulls of inhabitants.[2] In September 1942 Bergel complained to the Council of Elders that the daily death rates of Jews were going down. In order to create a chart that pleased him, they changed the chart from daily death rates to the total number of deaths.[3]

Bernstein, Elsa (1866–1949). An author noted for her comedy *The Children of the King*, Bernstein was designated "prominent" and sent to Theresienstadt despite her advanced age. She and her husband, Max Bernstein (1854–1925), hosted many notable European cultural leaders at their home, including Henrik Ibsen, Frank Wedekind, and Thomas Mann. She wrote a memoir of her experience in the camp, *Das Leben als Drama: Erinnerungen an Theresienstadt.*[4]

Bloch, Margarete (Grete; née Mosse) (1855–1943). Margarete Bloch was Eva's great-aunt. Her husband, Max Bloch (1852–1933), was a businessman. Their grandson, Konrad Bloch (1912–2000), won the

Nobel Prize for physiology in 1964. Eva recorded Margarete Bloch's death in Theresienstadt on 31 January 1943.

Corinth, Lovis (1858–1925). A German painter in Berlin, Corinth painted for many wealthy families, including Bianca and Richard Israel. He painted Richard in 1899. The Israels helped Corinth secure additional portrait commissions. Eva found the divide between her family as patron of the arts and Nazi camp inhabitants difficult to bridge when she thought about Corinth painting her family members.[5]

Danziger, Alfred (1895–1979). Alfred Danziger married Eva's sister, Hilde Mosse. After the war, the Danzigers moved to California.

Dunant, Paul (1901–1973). Dunant first visited Theresienstadt on 6 April 1945, as part of an International Red Cross delegation.[6] SS officers, including Adolf Eichmann, oversaw the Red Cross inspection. Eva saw him return on 4 May 1945, when he placed the camp under the protection of the Red Cross. On 7 May 1945 Dunant proclaimed in French and German that the Third Reich had surrendered unconditionally.[7]

Duse, Eleonora (1858–1924). An Italian actress known for her ability to play roles penned by Gabriele d'Annunzio and Henrik Ibsen. Duse died in Pittsburgh.[8] In Theresienstadt, Eva compares the beauty of one of her delousing guards to Duse.

Eppstein, Paul (1902–1944). The head of the Theresienstadt Jewish Council of Elders or "self-administration"; Eppstein was the spokesman for the council with the SS. On 27 September 1944 the SS murdered Eppstein in the Small Fortress within Theresienstadt. Eva suspects that he was killed for trying to tell the Red Cross about the real conditions of the camp during its inspection in the summer of 1944.

Grahammer, (Johann) Hans (1900–1955). A Gestapo inspector in Augsburg who told Eva she would have light office and canteen work when she was deported East.[9] Eva comments that she learned from Grahammer that "every single word of the Gestapo was a lie." In January 1948 Grahammer was questioned about the activities of his superiors.[10] In 1953 he was investigated along with other members of the Munich Gestapo office and sentenced to eight months in prison for the 1942 beating of the physicist Dr. Oskar Cossmann.

Grote, Andreas (1929–2015). Noack-Mosse consulted with historian George Mosse about their shared family history for a 1977 Ullstein publishing house exhibit coordinated by Andreas Grote.[11] Grote and Noack-Mosse worked together to fully represent the importance of the Mosse family for Berlin on the occasion of the hundredth anniversary of Ullstein Verlag. The Mosse and Ullstein publishers were professional rivals, but the families inhabited the same Berlin social circles.[12]

Hartleben, Otto Erich (1864–1905). A German poet and uncle of Moritz Noack, Eva's husband. Hartleben's work satirized the morals and standards of middle-class German society.[13] When the Gestapo questioned Moritz about his family medical history he was tempted to answer that there was a history of mental illness because there was a poet in the family.

Heindl, Rudolf (sometimes spelled Haindl) (1922–1948). Heindl arrived from Vienna as SS-Scharführer to Theresienstadt camp inspector Bergel.[14] He had a fierce reputation in the camp for showing up where he was not expected and personally conducting searches of prisoners. Heindl oversaw arrivals and deportations from the ghetto. Heindl left Theresienstadt on 2 or 3 May 1945 and was arrested two years later in Salzburg. He was executed in September 1948.

Hirsch, Else (1878–1943). One of Noack-Mosse's aunts in Berlin, Else married Paul Hirsch, a lawyer. Her parents were Leonore Mosse (1841–1909) and Emil Cohn (1832–1905), a business partner of Rudolf Mosse until 1884. Eva learned on 24 February 1945 that Else Hirsch had been deported to Auschwitz in 1943.

Hirsch, Jobst (1863–1943). Married to Eva's aunt Toni, Jobst Hirsch was an estate holder. Jobst and Toni Hirsch went to Theresienstadt on the same transport as Richard and Bianca Israel and Else and Paul Hirsch. In her "death dates" list, Eva records Jobst as dying on 18 January 1944. Elisabeth Kraus records Jobst and Toni's deaths as occurring in 1943, the same year they were deported.[15]

Hirsch, Paul (1866–1943). Married to Eva's aunt Else, Paul Hirsch was a lawyer. He died of dysentery in Theresienstadt in March 1943. Eva learned about his fate from the same camp inhabitant who told her about Else Hirsch's deportation.

Hirsch, Toni (Antonie) (1873–1943). Toni Hirsch was Eva's aunt and was married to Jobst Hirsch. Her parents were Leonore Mosse (1841–1909) and Emil Cohn (1832–1905), a business partner of Rudolf Mosse until 1884. Eva records her Aunt Toni as having died on 16 January 1944, two days before her husband Jobst. Again, Kraus records the couple as passing away in 1943.

Hirsch, Vivianne. Great-granddaughter of Leonore Cohn (Mosse), granddaughter of Paul and Else Hirsch, daughter of Günther and Wally Hirsch. Günther was Bianca Israel's nephew. Eva spent time with Vivianne Hirsch in Munich in 1973.

Israel, Bianca (née Cohn) (b. 1870). Bianca Israel was the daughter of Leonore Mosse (1841–1909) and Emil Cohn (1832–1905). She married Richard Israel in 1891. Bianca Israel went to Switzerland before the war ended, on 5 February 1945, on a transport of twelve hundred prisoners from Theresienstadt.[16]

Israel, Richard (1869–1943). Husband to Bianca Israel, Richard Israel had fought in the First World War, serving as adjutant to General Paul von Hindenburg (1847–1934). Though the Nazis initially excluded World War I veterans from anti-Jewish legislation, that exception was eliminated during the Second World War, and even decorated war veterans were deported to camps like Theresienstadt.

Kantorowicz, Ernst Hartwig (1895–1963). Author of *The King's Two Bodies*, Kantorowicz was a scholar whose work focused on medieval theology and Friedrich II.[17] Eva mentions Ernst Hartwig because he was the son of Clara Kantorowicz (1862–1943), an aunt of Eva's friend Dr. Gertrud Kantorowicz.

Kantorowicz, Gertrud (Kanto) (1876–1945). Attempted to flee to Switzerland in the summer of 1942 with her seventy-five-year-old aunt, Clara Kantorowicz. They were caught and sent to Bregenz. Eva called her "Kanto" and spent many evenings in conversation with her about art history and the end of their captivity in Theresienstadt. Kanto, an art historian, did not make it to the end of the war but died in April 1945, weeks before the liberation she and Eva so frequently discussed.

Keller, Gottfried (1819–1890). Keller was a Swiss poet and novelist known for his literary realism. Noack-Mosse reads his Zurich short stories while in Theresienstadt. This book and her blanket on the kitchen floor of her room are two of her reminders of home.

Laband, Paul (1838–1918). Paul Laband studied law in Breslau, Heidelberg, and Berlin. In 1872 he was appointed as a legal scholar to the University of Strasbourg. He was known for his 1883 publication *Das Staatsrecht des Deutschen Reiches,* or *The Constitutional Law of the German Reich.*[18] Noack-Mosse's mother, Regina, was Paul Laband's niece.

Lachmann-Mosse, Hans (1885–1944). Hans Lachmann-Mosse was Eva's uncle and married Felicia Mosse in October 1909. Lachmann-Mosse ran the Mosse publishing house, which Felicia Mosse inherited from her father, Rudolf. He escaped Nazi Germany and went to California where he died in 1944. His youngest son, George L. Mosse, received a copy of Noack-Mosse's Theresienstadt manuscript after the war, when he was a professor of history at the University of Iowa.

Levin, Julius (1894–1943) and Erna (1900–1943). Julius and Erna Levin were Noack-Mosse's cousins.[19] The couple were deported East from Theresienstadt on a worker's transport in October 1943 and were not heard from again. Eva describes Julius as a doctor. He would have been a cousin on her mother's side of the family.

Mann, Heinrich (1871–1950). Author Heinrich Mann was the older brother of Thomas Mann. Heinrich published *Professor Unrat oder das Ende eines Tyrannen* in 1905. His novel was later adapted into the film *Der blaue Engel* starring Marlene Dietrich in 1930.[20] In 1940 Mann left Germany for the United States. He lived in Hollywood and worked as screenwriter for Warner Brothers.

Mann, Klaus (1906–1949). Klaus Mann was Thomas Mann's son and a noted German author. He published *Mephisto* in 1936.[21] He arrived in Theresienstadt as a U.S. soldier on 19 May 1945. Noack-Mosse told him that his aunt Mimi (Maria Kanová [1866–1947]) had already left the camp and traveled to Prague. Kanová and Heinrich Mann divorced in 1928 after fourteen years of marriage.

Mann, Thomas (1875–1955). Thomas Mann won the Nobel Prize in Literature in 1929.[22] He published many important German novels, including *Buddenbrooks* (1901) and *Der Zauberberg* (1924). Mann left Germany in February 1933 for Czechoslovakia and then emigrated to the United States in 1939. He did not return to Europe again until 1947. His son, Klaus Mann, met Noack-Mosse in Theresienstadt at the end of the Second World War.

Mayser, Marga Helene (1913–1998). Marga Mayser was the daughter of the hat manufacturer Alfred Mayser.[23] Marga dated an Aryan, the pilot Hannes Karl Trauloft (1912–1995), during the war. With the collapse of the Third Reich, the couple wed. In 1951 they relocated to Munich with their daughter.

Meyer, Pauline (1874–1942). Pauline Meyer arrived in Theresienstadt as the widow of Richard Meyer (1865–1939), a professor of chemistry. She had a Swiss visa but had obtained it after the Third Reich banned emigration. Eva learned in Theresienstadt that Pauline Meyer had died in a camp barracks.

Modersohn-Becker, Paula (1876–1907). A German painter who helped pioneer expressionism, Modersohn-Becker died at the age of thirty-one. While in Theresienstadt, Eva read through her letters in order to escape back into German high culture and a "different world for a few minutes." Along with Modersohn-Becker's letters Eva brought a copy of *David Copperfield* with her to Theresienstadt.

Mosse, Albert (1846–1925). Albert was Rudolf Mosse's brother. Albert trained as a lawyer. In the 1880s he was invited to travel to Japan to help draft the Japanese state law code. Albert Mosse's work for Japan led the Japanese government to insist that his daughter, Martha Mosse, be designated "prominent" and sent to Theresienstadt rather than directly to a death camp.

Mosse, Felicia (1888–1972). Felicia Mosse was Noack-Mosse's aunt and the adopted daughter of Rudolf Mosse and Emilie Loewenstein (1851–1924). Like her husband, Hans Lachmann-Mosse, Felicia escaped the Third Reich. She moved first to Switzerland, then to France, and eventually to the United States. Felicia and Hans separated when they went into exile.[24]

Mosse, George L. (1918–1999). The rise of Nazism led George Lachmann-Mosse to leave Germany in 1933. He traveled to the United States in 1939. He obtained his PhD in history from Harvard in 1946. Eva

Noack-Mosse sent George her Theresienstadt memoir in October 1954 and asked for his help getting the work published and translated. George L. Mosse at the time was a professor at the University of Iowa. In 1955 he began a teaching and publishing career at the University of Wisconsin–Madison. Mosse published extensively in early modern and modern European history.

Mosse, Hilde (1904–1998). Hilde Mosse was Eva's youngest sister. Her parents were Regina Laband (1878–1938) and Max Mosse. She and her husband, Alfred Danziger, moved to California after the Second World War.

Mosse, Käte (1900–1989). Käte Mosse was Eva's oldest sister. Her husband, Leonardo Olschki, was a literary scholar. Like her sister Hilde, Käte left Europe for the United States after the Second World War.

Mosse, Markus (1808–1865). Markus Mosse was a physician in Graetz and Eva's great-grandfather. He and his wife, Ulrike Wolff (1813–1888), had seven sons and seven daughters, including Eva's grandfather Theodor and George's grandfather Rudolf.

Mosse, Martha (1884–1977). Dr. Martha Mosse arrived in Theresienstadt from Berlin on 17 June 1943.[25] She was the daughter of Albert Mosse, who helped develop the Japanese legal code, and her mother was Caroline Meyer (1859–1934). Martha was Eva Noack-Mosse's aunt and, like her father, she was a lawyer. She testified against Gottlob Berger, general of the Waffen-SS, in February 1948. She was designated "prominent" in the ghetto and remained in Germany after the war.

Mosse, Max (1873–1936). Max Mosse was a Berlin physician, professor of medicine, and Eva's father. During his career, Max published on several medical topics, including sickness and society, microbiology, and pathology. He and his wife, Regina, had three daughters: Käte, Eva, and Hilde.

Mosse, Regina (née Laband) (1878–1938). Regina Laband was Noack-Mosse's mother. Regina's father was the lawyer Paul Laband. Her husband was Max Mosse. Together she and Max had three daughters, Käte, Eva, and Hilde.

Mosse, Rudolf (1843–1920). Great-uncle to Eva Noack-Mosse and grandfather to George L. Mosse. Rudolf Mosse established the *Berliner*

Tageblatt as a powerful voice in German politics. Rudolf adopted
Felicia Mosse in May 1893. His wife, Emilie Loewenstein, finalized
her adoption of Felicia in 1919.[26] Felicia inherited the *Berliner Tage-*
blatt and Mosse publishing interests across Europe.

Mosse, Theodor (1842–1916). Theodor Mosse was one of Rudolf Mosse's
six brothers. In Berlin, he ran a clothing firm. Noack-Mosse mentions her grandfather Theodor in the context of the place of the
Mosse family in German society before the Nuremberg Laws were
implemented.

Noack, Moritz Eduard (1896–1980). Eva and Moritz Eduard Noack wed
in 1934, before the Nuremberg Laws prohibiting Jews and Aryans
from marrying went into effect. Moritz and Eva lived together in
Berlin until 1941. From Berlin they moved to a Bavarian village,
Oberstdorf, to await the end of the Third Reich. In January 1945
Moritz was summoned to the Gestapo office in Augsburg to report
for forced labor. He was spared this duty and returned home. Eva
thinks of Moritz often during her time in Theresienstadt. From the
camp, Eva attempts to communicate with Moritz via postcard, but
only one of her missives made it home. She reunited with Moritz on
7 July 1945.

Olschki, Leonardo (1885–1961). Leonardo Olschki was a literary scholar
and Noack-Mosse's brother-in-law. He married Eva's eldest sister,
Käte Mosse. Leonardo taught in Rome and in California. He focused
on the Italian Renaissance and published historical articles in Latin,
Italian, German, English, and French. In 1950 he refused to sign the
loyalty oath at Berkeley.

Panofsky, Dora (née Mosse) (1885–1965). Born Dora Mosse, she was the
daughter of Albert Mosse and Caroline Meyer. Dora's husband was
the art historian Erwin Panofsky. Together they had two sons, Hans
and Wolfgang. Dora was Martha Mosse's sister.

Panofsky, Erwin (1892–1968). Erwin Panofsky was an art historian and
married to Dora Mosse. A prolific author, Erwin wrote books on
the Renaissance, visual arts, Albrecht Dürer, tomb sculpture, and
the role of ideas in art theory.

Princip, Gavrilo (1894–1918). Gavrilo Princip shot and killed Archduke
Franz Ferdinand in Sarajevo on 28 June 1914. The assassination

sparked a diplomatic crisis that led into the First World War. Princip was arrested and incarcerated at Theresienstadt, where he died in 1918 of tuberculosis.

Rahm, Karl (1907–1947). Karl Rahm was the last SS-Obersturmführer of Theresienstadt. During deportations, Rahm would occasionally release healthy-looking Jews from the trains heading East.[27] Rahm left the camp on 5 May 1945 and fled into Austria, where he was arrested by the United States in November. He was executed on 3 April 1947.[28]

Schiepan, Käthe (née Hirsch) (1872–1942). Käthe Schiepan was a physician and Gershom Scholem's aunt.[29] Her sister was Betty Scholem, Gershom Scholem's mother. Käthe married an Aryan colleague who asked for a divorce in 1933 so that he could marry a fellow Aryan. As a result, Käthe was deported to Thereisenstadt and killed.[30]

Scholem, Gershom (1897–1982). Gershom Scholem was born into a German Jewish family in Berlin in 1897. Scholem established the study of Jewish mysticism through analyses of kabbalistic literature, mysticism, Zionism, Jewish historiography, as well as studies of contemporary Jewish communities.[31] He left Germany for Palestine in 1923 and taught at the Hebrew University of Jerusalem for the rest of his life.

Seidl, Siegfried (1911–1947). Theresienstadt Oberscharführer from 1941 to 1943. In 1943 he was transferred to Bergen-Belsen. Seidl was known as a sadistic man and virulent anti-Semite by camp inhabitants. Eva hears a rumor in April 1945 that the former Oberscharführer has called the camp. After the war Seidl was sentenced to death and executed in Vienna.[32]

Stahmer, Otto (1879–1968). A German defense lawyer who was Eva and Moritz's neighbor in Oberstdorf. Stahmer is best known for defending Hermann Göring (1893–1946) during the Nuremberg trials after the Second World War. Stahmer's questioning of Göring on "living space" and the "master race" offered the former Luftwaffe commander a podium from which to defend Nazi policy and actions during the trial.[33]

Stock, Erna. Martha Mosse's partner in Berlin. Erna was not Jewish and had difficulty getting a visa to leave Germany. Martha did not want to leave her behind and so stayed. Erna Stock stood with Martha through the Nazi period. In 1945 Martha wrote to her sister Dora

Panofsky that "therefore she naturally cannot get any work and after my departure the Gestapo visited often to conduct searches."[34] On 5 June 1945 Eva notes that Martha is eager to get back to Berlin to see Erna.

Strauss, Elsa (1875–1945). An old friend of Noack-Mosse's who lived in the Magdeburger barracks in Theresienstadt. She and her husband, Hermann Strauss (1868–1944), arrived in the camp in 1942. Elsa Strauss was spared transport to Auschwitz when her husband died of a heart attack. Elsa did not live to see the end of the war, dying a few weeks before Theresienstadt prisoners from Berlin were sent home.

Von Salomon, Ernst (1902–1972). Participated in the assassination of Walther Rathenau on 24 June 1922. Von Salomon was sentenced to five years in prison. He was active in anti-Weimar activities throughout the 1920s but did not join the Nazi Party.[35] Even so, the regime recommended his books. After the war von Salomon published *The Questionnaire*, which challenged the efficacy of Allied denazification policies. Eva Noack-Mosse read this work in 1952 and was disturbed by von Salomon's portrayal of his actions during the Rathenau assassination.

Zuckmayer, Amalie Friederike Auguste (1869–1947). Amalie Zuckmayer was Carl Zuckmayer's mother and a friend of the Noack family.[36] She and her husband, Carl, were forced to leave their home in Mainz due to Allied firebombing. They took refuge in Oberstdorf, where Eva and her husband lived after they left Berlin in 1941.

Zuckmayer, Carl (1896–1977). Praised Eva's memoir as being well written. Eva reports to George that he "found it excellent." Carl Zuckmayer penned the screenplay for *Der blaue Engel* based on Heinrich Mann's *Professor Unrat*. He also wrote the play *The Captain of Köpenick*. In 1966 Zuckmayer published an autobiography titled *Als wär's ein Stück von mir*.[37]

Zülzer, Gertrude (Trude) (1873–1968). A German painter and one of Eva's roommates in Theresienstadt, along with Elsa Strauss. Zülzer had known Eva's parents before the Second World War and arrived in Theresienstadt three years before Eva. Trude Zülzer painted Eva in June 1945 in exchange for 160 grams of oatmeal.

Notes

Foreword

1. Works that have made use of Noack-Mosse include Renate Bridenthal, Atina Grossmann, and Marion A. Kaplan, *When Biology Became Destiny: Women in Weimar and Nazi Germany* (New York: New Feminist Library, 1984); Sybil Milton, "Women and the Holocaust," in *The Nazi Holocaust, Part 6. Victims of the Holocaust*, ed. Michael Marrus, 2:631–67 (Meckler: Westport and London, 1989); Anna Hájková, "Mutmassungen über Deutsche Juden: Alte Menschen aus Deutschland im Theresienstädter Ghetto," in *Alltag im holocaust: Jüdisches leben im Grossdeutschen reich, 1941–1945, schriftenreihe der Vierteljahrshefte für zeitgeschichte*, ed. Andrea Löw, Doris L. Bergen, and Anna Hájková, 179–98 (Munich: Oldenbourg, 2013).

2. Maximilian Strnad, "The Fortune of Survival: Intermarried German Jews in the Dying Breath of the 'Thousand-Year Reich,'" *Dapim: Studies on the Holocaust* 29, no. 3 (2015): 173–96.

3. Marion A. Kaplan, *Between Dignity and Despair: Jewish Life in Nazi Germany* (New York: Oxford University Press, 1998).

Introduction

1. For biographical information on Eva Noack-Mosse see the Deutsches Literatur Archiv in Marbach (www.dla-marbach.de/index.php?id=448&ADISDB =PE&WEB=JA&ADISOI=00052215). On the Mosse family, see Elisabeth Kraus, *Die Familie Mosse: Deutsch-jüdisches Bürgertum im 19. und 20. Jahrhundert* (Munich: Verlag C.H. Beck, 1999).

2. For Leonardo Olschki's obituary, see George L. Mosse Collection, box 1, folder 23, Leo Baeck Institute. Käte sent the obituary to Mosse "for the family album." Between 1932 and 1938, before they left for California, the Olschkis lived in Rome, where Leonardo was a visiting professor at the University of Rome (Kraus, *Die Familie Mosse*, 539). Olschki was a renowned scholar of the

Italian Renaissance. He published in Latin, Italian, German, English, and French. In the United States, he gained fame for refusing to sign the 1950 loyalty oath at the University of California, Berkeley. See also Robert E. Lerner's discussion of Olschki and Kantorowicz's friendship in *Ernst Kantorowicz: A Life* (Princeton: Princeton University Press, 2017), 270–71.

3.   Noack-Mosse to Mosse, 26 July 1976, George L. Mosse Collection, AR 25137, box 38, folder 7, Leo Baeck Institute.

4.   It was not unusual for Germans to use a hyphenated last name. For example, Hans Lachmann, George L. Mosse's father, hyphenated his name to Lachmann-Mosse after he married Felicia Mosse in 1910. See George L. Mosse, *Confronting History: A Memoir* (Madison: University of Wisconsin Press, 2000), 25–26.

5.   Matthew Stibbe, *Women in the Third Reich* (New York: Oxford University Press, 2003), 67–70.

6.   Marion Kaplan, *Between Dignity and Despair: Jewish Life in Nazi Germany* (New York: Oxford University Press, 1998), 93.

7.   See Beate Meyer's study of more than one hundred mixed couples, *"Jüdische Mischlinge": Rassenpolitik und Verfolgungserfahrungen, 1933–1945* (Hamburg: Dölling und Galitz, 1999). Bertolt Brecht described the pressures placed on mixed couples in his play *The Jewish Wife*. See *The Jewish Wife and Other Short Plays*, trans. Eric Bentley (New York: Grove Press, 1965).

8.   Kaplan, *Between Dignity and Despair*, 93. Also cited by Stibbe, *Women in the Third Reich*, 70.

9.   The sluice doubled as a staging barracks for deportations. See Gonda Redlich, *The Terezin Diary of Gonda Redlich*, ed. Saul S. Friedman, trans. Laurence Kutler (Lexington: University of Kentucky Press, 1992), 80. In the camp, "sluiced" (*geschleust*) became slang for "stolen" because as they processed incoming inmates, the Nazi and Czech guards appropriated their valuables (Susan E. Cernyak-Spatz, *Protective Custody: Prisoner 34042* [Cortland, NY: N and S Publishers, 2005], 88). Compared to the processing of previous years, Eva's was quick. Norbert Troller remembered new camp inhabitants being held in the sluice for several days before being released into the general population. He was deported to Theresienstadt in 1942 (*Theresienstadt: Hitler's Gift to the Jews*, ed. Joel Shatzky, trans. Susan E. Cernyak-Spatz [Chapel Hill: University of North Carolina Press, 1991], 55–59).

10.   Zdenek Lederer, *Ghetto Theresienstadt* (New York: Howard Fertig, 1983), 250–51. See also notes throughout when Eva cites specific figures.

11.   Camp conditions were designed to maximize the death rate. When informed in August 1942 that between seventy-five and one hundred individuals died every day at Theresienstadt, camp Oberscharführer Siegfried Seidl stated, "The clock ticks well." See Lederer, *Ghetto Theresienstadt*, 49.

12.   Philipp Manes, *As If It Were Life: A WWII Diary from the Theresienstadt Ghetto* (New York: Palgrave Macmillan, 2009), 70.

13.   In addition to German Jews, transports from Czechoslovakia, Austria, Luxembourg, and Poland arrived in 1942 (H. G. Adler, *Theresienstadt, 1941–1945: The Face of a Coerced Community*, ed. Amy Loewenhaar-Blauweiss, trans. Belinda Cooper [Cambridge: Cambridge University Press, 2017], 33–34).

14.   Eva's great-aunt Margarete (Grete) Bloch (née Mosse) died in Theresienstadt in 1943. Margarete's grandson, Konrad Bloch, won the Nobel Prize for physiology in 1964. See Kraus, *Die Familie Mosse*, 281, 557.

15.   Bianca Israel (née Cohn) is included in a list of liberated Theresienstadt inmates published in "Befreite aus Theresienstadt," *Aufbau: Nachrichtenblatt des German-Jewish Club* 11, no. 7 (1945): 28; cf. "Also miscellaneous personal documents including Jewish identity card," 6, Wiener Library Document 504d/1. Bianca Israel was related to both George and Eva Mosse. She was the daughter of Leonore Mosse (1841–1909) and Emil Cohn (1832–1905). In 1891 she married Richard Israel.

16.   Martha Mosse arrived in Theresienstadt on 17 June 1943, on transport number 13,352. She was designated as "prominent" because of the intervention of the Japanese government and the work of Wilhelm Solf, Japanese chargé d'affaires in Berlin. See Kraus, *Die Familie Mosse*, 581. Before Martha was sent to Theresienstadt she worked for the Jüdische Gemeinde zu Berlin (the Jewish Community of Berlin, forced by the Reich to rename itself the Jüdische Kultusvereinigung zu Berlin on 2 April 1941. See Beate Meyer, "Gratwanderung zwischen Verantwortung und Verstrickung: Die Reichsvereinigung der Juden in Deutschland und die Jüdische Gemeinde zu Berlin 1938–1945," in *Juden in Berlin 1938–1945: Begleitband zur gleichnamigen Ausstellung in der Stiftung 'Neue Synagoge Berlin—Centrum Judaicum,' Mai bis August 2000*, ed. Beate Meyer and Hermann Simon [Berlin: Philo Verlagsgesellschaft, 2000], 291–337). In 1952, she was accused of turning individuals over to the Gestapo while coordinating housing and food ration coupons. She was acquitted of all charges.

17.   Kraus, *Die Familie Mosse*, 581.

18.   Gertrud Kantorowicz was Ernst Kantorwicz's cousin. See Lerner, *Ernst Kantorowicz*, 73. See also Robert Lerner, "The Secret Germany of Gertrud

Kantorowicz," in *A Poet's Reich: Politics and Culture in the George Circle*, ed. Melissa S. Lane and Martin A. Ruehl (Rochester, NY: Camden House, 2011), 56–77.

19. See Manes, *As If It Were Life*, and Ilse Weber, *Dancing on a Powder Keg*, trans. Michael Schwartz (Charlottetown: Bunim and Bannigan, 2016). Noack-Mosse's diary is also unique among other survivor accounts by authors who survived after deportation to Auschwitz (see, for example, Ruth Klüger, *Weiter Leben: Eine Jugend* [Göttingen: Wallstein Verlag, 1992], and Cernyak-Spatz, *Protective Custody*) or that end with the cessation of hostilities (such as Eva Roubickova's *We're Alive and Life Goes On: A Theresienstadt Diary*, trans. Virginia Euwer Wolff [New York: Henry Holt, 1998], and Elsa Bernstein's *Das Leben als Drama: Erinnerungen an Theresienstadt*, ed. Rita Bake and Birgit Kiupel [Hamburg: Landeszentrale für politische Bildung, 2005]).

20. Eva Noack-Mosse, "Tagebuch einer Überlebenden," *Frankfurter Hefte* 7, no. 3 (1952): 163–64. Eva often wrote for a wide audience; for instance, she also published articles in Zurich's *Die Tat*, including "Ein Huhn reist ins Engadin" (3 June 1972) and "Wette mit mir: Ein neues Beschäftigungsspiel" (25 April 1975).

21. Noack-Mosse to Mosse, 5 October 1954, George L. Mosse Collection, AR 25137, box 38, folder 7, Leo Baeck Institute. Noack-Mosse's correspondence with George L. Mosse is translated as an appendix of this volume.

22. Noack-Mosse to Mosse, 31 October 1973, George L. Mosse Collection, AR 25137, box 38, folder 7, Leo Baeck Institute.

23. Noack-Mosse to Mosse, 10 August 1973, George L. Mosse Collection, AR 25137, box 38, folder 7, Leo Baeck Institute.

24. See Werner Mosse's comment in Albert and Lina Mosse, *Fast wie mein eigen Vaterland: Briefe aus Japan 1886–1889*, ed. Shirō Ishii, Ernst Lokowandt, and Yūkichi Sakai (Munich: Iudicium Verlag, 1995), 36.

25. George L. Mosse Collection, AR 25137, box 38, folder 7, Leo Baeck Institute; Wiener Library Document 504d/1. A scan of Eva Noack-Mosse's typescript is available via www.lbi.org/digibaeck.

Last Days of Theresienstadt

1. For the English edition, see H. G. Adler, *Theresienstadt, 1941–1945: The Face of a Coerced Community*, ed. Amy Loewenhaar-Blauweiss, trans. Belinda Cooper (Cambridge: Cambridge University Press, 2017). Although Noack-Mosse here suggests Adler is cited as "Adler, *Theresienstadt*" in her manuscript,

he is in fact only referenced once by name, when she notes his documentation of the negotiations between the SS and the Red Cross. Throughout the text, Noack-Mosse's corroborating statistical statements as well as information she would learn after the war have been italicized. These asides are an essential aspect of her testimony.

2. Paul Laband, *Das Staatsrecht des Deutschen Reiches* (Freiburg: Mohr, 1883). A digital copy is available at www.deutschestextarchiv.de/book/view/laband _staatsrecht01_1876?p=11. Laband was a legal scholar at the University of Strasbourg. See Johannes Wilhelm, *Die Lehre von Staat und Gesetz von Paul Laband* (Cologne: A. Bothmann, 1967).

3. See Elisabeth Kraus, *Die Familie Mosse: Deutsch-jüdisches Bürgertum im 19. und 20. Jahrhundert* (Munich: Beck, 1999), 99, 242, 259. See also the digital collection of Gebrüder Mosse artifacts at the Jüdisches Museum Berlin website: http://objekte.jmberlin.de/view/objectimage.seam?uuid=jmb-obj-364066 &cid=450024.

4. Rudolf Mosse was George L. Mosse's grandfather.

5. For a virtual tour of the Mosse Palais and its environs see the documentary *Die Voßstraße*, directed by Christoph Neubauer (Dar Es Salaam: Christoph Neubauer Verlag, 2008), DVD.

6. Visit Yale's Avalon Project for translations of Dr. Otto Strahmer's interrogation of Hermann Göring during the Nuremberg trials (http://avalon.law .yale.edu/imt/03-14-46.asp).

7. On the Aktion OT, see Franz W. Seidler, *Die Organisation Todt: Bauen für Staat und Wehrmacht, 1938–1945* (Koblenz: Bernard und Graefe, 1987); Anson Rabinbach and Sander L. Gilman, *The Third Reich Sourcebook* (Berkeley: University of California Press, 2013), 485.

8. See United States Holocaust Memorial Museum, "Ohrdruf," *Holocaust Encyclopedia*, www.ushmm.org/wlc/en/article.php?ModuleId=10006131.

9. The Allies accepted Germany's unconditional surrender on 8 May 1945.

10. See Marita Krauss, ed., *Rechte Karrieren in München: Von der Weimarer Zeit bis in die Nachkriegsjahre* (Munich: Volk Verlag, 2010), 220–24.

11. Noack-Mosse continues to call the greater Theresienstadt area "Czechoslovakia," though the Nazis annexed the Sudetenland in 1938 and invaded the rest of the country in 1939.

12. Of the 57,628 individuals deported East from Theresienstadt, only 6,008 survived according to a 2000 Stockholm International Conference on the Holocaust. See Susan E. Cernyak-Spatz, *Protective Custody: Prisoner 34042* (Cortland, NY: N and S Publishers, 2005), 91.

13. There was a total of fifty-two people on Eva's train to Theresienstadt (Alfred Gottwaldt and Diana Schulle, *Die "Judendeportationen" aus dem Deutschen Reich, 1941–1945: Eine kommentierte Chronologie* [Wiesbaden: Marix Verlag, 2005], 467).

14. Vauban (1633–1707) was considered an architectural genius when it came to the construction of fortifications. Though Theresienstadt was in fact built by Austrian Emperor Joseph II (1741–1790) after Vauban's time, between 1780 and 1790, it still followed Vauban's model for defensive structures. Joseph II named the fortress for his mother, the Empress Maria Theresa (1717–1780).

15. National Socialist Germany undertook the creation of a propaganda film set in Theresienstadt designed to show that concentration camps did not violate international law. The film was never completed or distributed; see *The Fuehrer Gives the Jews a City*, directed by Kurt Gerron (Los Angeles: Seventh Art Release, 2010), DVD. On the origins of the film and how it was produced, see H. G. Adler, *Die verheimlichte Wahrheit: Theresienstädter Dokumente* (Tübingen: Mohr, 1958), 324–52. Gonda Redlich described an earlier film on 9 November 1942: "They are making a film. Jewish actors, happy, satisfied, happy faces in the film, only in the film" (*The Terezin Diary of Gonda Redlich*, ed. Saul S. Friedman, trans. Laurence Kutler [Lexington: University of Kentucky Press, 1992], 83).

16. Eleonora Duse was an Italian actress known for her roles in plays penned by Gabriele d'Annunzio (1863–1938) and Henrik Ibsen (1828–1906). Duse died in Pittsburgh.

17. Horst Uhr, *Lovis Corinth* (Los Angeles: University of California Press, 1990), 116. Lovis Corinth painted Richard Israel in 1899 and began a painting of Bianca Israel the same year but destroyed it before it was completed; Richard and Bianca also helped Corinth secure portrait commissions (Uhr, *Lovis Corinth*, 117, 124). See also Peter Kropmanns, "So viel Geld für ein bisschen bemalte Leinwand," *Frankfurter Allgemeine Zeitung*, 19 July 2008, www.faz.net/aktuell /feuilleton/kunstmarkt/galerien/lovis-corinth-und-der-kunsthandel-so-viel -geld-fuer-ein-bisschen-bemalte-leinwand-1665019.html.

18. See United States Holocaust Memorial Museum, "Theresienstadt: Final Weeks, Liberation, and Postwar Trials," *Holocaust Encyclopedia*, www.ushmm .org/wlc/en/article.php?ModuleId=10007505.

19. Joseph von Eichendorff (1788–1857), along with German painters Caspar David Friedrich (1774–1840) and the Norwegian artist Johan Christian Dahl (1788–1857), helped found German romanticism. On Eichendorff's life and work see Hermann Korte, *Joseph von Eichendorff* (Reinbek bei Hamburg: Rowohlt, 2000).

20. In 1940 Theresienstadt had a population of thirty-seven hundred living in 219 homes and could house thirty-five hundred soldiers. Germany took over the town in 1941 and transformed it into a concentration camp (Zdenek Lederer, *Ghetto Theresienstadt* [New York: Howard Fertig, 1983], 2, 14). The first transport of prisoners, conveying 342 young men, arrived in Theresienstadt at 4:30 a.m. on 24 November 1941 (Wolfgang Benz, *Theresienstadt: Eine Geschichte von Täuschung und Vernichtung* [Munich: C.H. Beck, 2013], 265).

21. The Nazis designated their occupied portion of Czechoslovakia the Protectorate of Bohemia and Moravia. On 10 October 1941 Heydrich decided to use Theresienstadt as a holding area for Jews living in the Protectorate. The town was selected because it was easy to guard and was conveniently located for further transportation East. On 19 October 1941 the Jüdische Kultusvereinigung zu Berlin confirmed that Theresienstadt would be a staging ground for Protectorate Jews. Adler notes that it is unclear where the idea to establish a Jewish camp in the Protectorate originated (*Theresienstadt*, 15, 22, 51).

22. Adler calculates that between 24 November 1941 and 20 April 1945 a total of 140,937 people were deported to Theresienstadt (*Theresienstadt*, 33–34).

23. Benjamin Murmelstein (1905–1989) was a rabbi from Vienna. He became the sole remaining Jewish elder in Theresienstadt on 27 September 1944, when Paul Eppstein was arrested and summarily shot in the Theresienstadt "Small Fortress." Murmelstein was the only Jewish elder to survive the Holocaust. In May 1945, when the SS left Theresienstadt, Karl Rahm, the last SS-Obersturmführer of Theresienstadt, discussed transferring the camp over to Murmelstein (Adler, *Theresienstadt*, 154–55, 174).

24. The International Committee of the Red Cross visited Theresienstadt on 23 June 1944. In preparation, German and Czech officials intensified transports to the East so the camp would not appear overcrowded. They also "beautified" the camp. It was following this visit that SS officials began production of *The Führer Gives the Jews a City*. The Red Cross visited again on 6 April 1945 (Adler, *Theresienstadt*, 145).

25. From 1942 through 1943, there were up to 563 doctors and up to 1,583 nurses in the camp. By 1944 these figures had declined to 120 practicing doctors and 257 nurses. See Adler, *Theresienstadt*, 452.

26. A total of eighty-seven thousand Theresienstadt inmates were transported to the East over the course of the war. Of these, Lederer estimates that at most 4 to 5 percent survived the journey and subsequent incarceration in concentration camps (*Ghetto Theresienstadt*, 199).

27. On Gertrud Kantorowicz and her attempted escape to the Swiss border, see Petra Zudrell, ed., *Der abgerissene Dialog: Die intellektuelle Beziehung Gertrud*

Kantorowicz—Margarete Susman oder Die Schweizer Grenze bei Hohenems als Endpunkt eines Fluchtversuchs (Innsbruck: StudienVerlag, 1999).

28. For more on Gertrud's attempted escape, see Lerner, *Ernst Kantorowicz*, 259–60. Gertrud Kantorowicz wrote poems while in the camp, including an epitaph for Clara, who died in 1943 (Alain Boureau, *Kantorowicz: Stories of a Historian* [Baltimore, MD: Johns Hopkins University Press, 2001], 44), that included the famous line "how quietly we kiss the beringed finger" (see Lerner, *Ernst Kantorowicz*, 60).

29. His name was Ernst Hartwig Kantorowicz. He published works on Kaiser Friedrich II and medieval political theology. For a discussion of his legacy, see Robert L. Benson, Ralph E. Giesey, and Margaret B. Sevcenko, "Defending Kantorowicz," as well as the reply by Robert Bartlett, *New York Review of Books*, 23 August 1992, www.nybooks.com/articles/1992/08/13/defending-kantorowicz.

30. Immorality was a concern of many in the camp. Gonda Redlich constantly worried about children having no moral examples to follow: "It is hard to offer a 100 percent moral education here, for lack of models. (For who doesn't carry off something?)" (*The Terezin Diary*, 84). During a 13 January 1944 trial of youths for stealing, one of them told Redlich, "Here life is different from normality. When we return to normality, we will become decent again" (*The Terezin Diary*, 140). See also Cernyak-Spatz, *Protective Custody*, 71–93, for a discussion of camp morality.

31. Günther Roth, *Max Webers deutsch-englische Familiengeschichte 1800–1950* (Tübingen: J.C.B. Mohr, 2001), 599.

32. Paula Modersohn-Becker was an important early expressionist painter. For a recent discussion of her paintings and letters, see John Colapinto, "Paula Modersohn-Becker: Modern Painting's Missing Piece," *New Yorker*, 29 October 2013, www.newyorker.com/books/page-turner/paula-modersohn-becker-modern-paintings-missing-piece.

33. Eva Noack-Mosse spells Elsa's name as Else in her memoir. For a list of prisoners designated "prominent," see Anna Hyndráková, Helena Krejčová, and Jana Svobodová, eds., *Prominenti v Ghettu Terezín (1942–1945)* (Prague: Ústav pro soudobé dějiny AV ČR, 1996).

34. *Jaarboek van de Maatschappij der Nederlandsche Letterkunde te Leiden* (Leiden: Brill, 1946), 132–41.

35. This is most likely the actress Henriette Sara Beck (Falkenstein) (1869–1945). See Hyndráková, Krejčová, and Svobodová, *Prominenti*, 126. After the war, Emmi Göring (1893–1973) published a memoir about her marriage to

Hermann Göring titled *An der Seite meines Mannes*, translated into English as *My Life with Göring* (London: David Bruce and Watson, 1972).

36. Kaiserliche Deutsche Gesandtschaft (von Holleben), Tokyo, to the Reichskanzler (von Caprivi), 13 April 1890; Martha Mosse, "Erinnerungen" (1963), Center for Jewish History, http://digital.cjh.org:80/R/-?func=dbin -jump-full&object_id=527178&silo_library=GEN01.

37. Part of Albert Mosse's correspondence has been published in *Fast wie mein eigen Vaterland* (Munich: Iudicium Verlag, 1995).

38. Jean-Pierre Chaline and Anne-Marie Sohn, eds., *Dictionnaire des parlementaires de Haute-Normandie sous la Troisième République, 1871–1940* (Rouen: Publications de l'Université de Rouen, 2000), 234; *Theresienstädter Gedenkbuch: Die Opfer der Judentransporte aus Deutschland nach Theresienstadt, 1942–1945* (Prague: Institut Theresienstädter Initiative, 2000), 324; Joachim Lilla, "Schneidhuber, August," in Staatsminister, leitende Verwaltungsbeamte und (NS-) Funktionsträger in Bayern 1918 bis 1945, https://verwaltungshandbuch .bayerische-landesbibliothek-online.de/schneidhuber-august; Elsa Bernstein, *Das Leben als Drama: Erinnerungen an Theresienstadt*, ed. Rita Bake and Birgit Kiupel (Hamburg: Landeszentrale für politische Bildung, 2005).

39. Here Noack-Mosse contrasts Martha's "prominent" living quarters with her own barracks. Because the Nazis had depopulated the camp over the preceding year, Eva eventually received more living space than those designated prominent earlier in the war, including Philipp Manes. German economic and class divisions were replicated in the camp, and tensions between national groups persisted. Manes complained about being associated with the Nazis just because he was a German speaker, considering that he had been deported to Theresienstadt. See Manes, *As If It Were Life: A WWII Diary from the Theresienstadt Ghetto* (New York: Palgrave Macmillan, 2009), 70.

40. Elsa and Hermann Strauss were married in 1899. Elsa survived the war but died in June 1945 before she could leave the camp. Hermann died in Theresienstadt (Adler, *Theresienstadt*, 214, 473). Berlin has erected a plaque in front of the house they shared from 1937 to 1942 to commemorate their charitable medical work. On Hermann Strauss, see also "Hermann Strauß (1868–1944)," Stadtarchiv Heilbronn, https://stadtarchiv.heilbronn.de/stadtge schichte/geschichte-a-z/s/strauss-hermann.html.

41. Trude is short for Gertrud. For a biography of Trude, see Max Bloch, "Gertrud und Margarete Zuelzer: Zwei Schwestern im Holocaust," *Aschkenas* 24, no. 1 (2014): 195–213, and Franziska Bogdanov, "Das Leben wird anders schauen nach dieser Schreckenszeit: Der Nachlass von Gertrud und Margarete

Zuelzer im Jüdischen Museum Berlin," *JMB Journal* 13 (2015): 40–41, https://issuu.com/jmb_journal/docs/jmb_journal_2015_-_2_druck/40.

42. Adler puts the figure at 139,594 (*Theresienstadt*, 775).

43. Adler breaks down camp survival rates by age groups and nationality (*Theresienstadt*, 775–78).

44. At the height of the typhoid epidemic there were seven thousand infections each month. In the camp a sign appeared on many buildings that read, "Never forget! Before eating, after every trip to the bathroom, wash your hands! Protect against contagion—typhoid—infection!" (Adler, *Theresienstadt*, 285–86, 454–55). There is debate about when the camp was hit by typhus and when by typhoid fever. For Adler, *Flecktyphus* or exanthematic typhus did not arrive until 1944 on a transport from Berlin (*Theresienstadt*, 461). Lederer also posits that the early outbreaks of disease were typhoid and resulted in 127 deaths out of 1,234 cases (*Ghetto Theresienstadt*, 138–40). See also Redlich, *The Terezin Diary*, 86–87.

45. The poor camp diet led to many hunger-related diseases, including osteoporosis, vitamin deficiencies, scurvy, stomatitis, and tachycardia.

46. Jews were not allowed to buy fresh produce, sugar, eggs, or chocolate with their ration cards during the war. A police order issued on 4 July 1940 in Berlin stated that Jews could only buy groceries between 4 and 5 p.m., by which time daily supplies would typically have sold out. Aryans received two pounds of potatoes per person per week, while Jews received one pound per person (Lisa Pine, *Nazi Family Policy, 1933–1945* [New York: Berg, 1997], 168).

47. The twelve hundred prisoners were selected for their health and their connections abroad (Lederer, *Ghetto Theresienstadt*, 174–75).

48. Adler measures the total number of children, not just *Reichsdeutschen*, and for his purposes he defines children as individuals under sixteen. He puts the percentage of children in the camp higher, at around 9.7 percent (*Theresienstadt*, 364).

49. Noack-Mosse arrived in the camp after most children had been deported. There are a number of works that feature the artwork and writing of Theresienstadt children, including Susan Goldman Rubin, *Fireflies in the Dark: The Story of Friedl Dicker-Brandeis and the Children of Terezin* (New York: Holiday House, 2000); Ursula Krause-Schmitt, Barbara Leissing, and Gottfried Schmidt, eds., *Kinder im KZ Theresienstadt—Zeichnungen, Gedichte, Texte: Katalog zur Ausstellung* (Frankfurt: Studienkreis Deutscher Widerstand, 2003); and Hana Volavková, ed., *I Never Saw Another Butterfly: Children's Drawings and Poems from Terezín Concentration Camp, 1942–1944* (New York: McGraw-Hill, 1976).

50.   In August 1943 Nazis deported five thousand Jews to Auschwitz from Theresienstadt and set them up in a "family camp" as a second "model" community for international observers. After six months, the Auschwitz family camp was emptied and everyone gassed (Redlich, *The Terezin Diary*, 130).

51.   There were many individuals who continued to educate children, including Friedl Dicker-Brandeis (1898–1944); see Volavková, *I Never Saw Another Butterfly*, xix–xx.

52.   Of the fifteen thousand children sent to Theresienstadt, only one hundred survived (Redlich, *The Terezin Diary*, vii).

53.   For a memoir of a German Hitler Youth member, see Alfons Heck, *A Child of Hitler: Germany in the Days When God Wore a Swastika* (Frederick, CO: Renaissance House, 1985).

54.   This trend holds for individuals over seventy years old until the end of 1945. The eldest camp survivor was ninety-six years old (Adler, *Theresienstadt*, 777).

55.   In September 1944, 4,019 inhabitants were sent out from the camp, and in October an additional 14,403 were put on transports. There were 17,565 total inhabitants in March 1945. Lederer calculates the total number of Germans sent to Theresienstadt in the fall of 1944 to be much lower than five thousand, 150 total (*Ghetto Theresienstadt*, 248–49).

56.   Eva here underestimates how many detainees arrived at the ghetto. Adler puts the total number of prisoners arriving in Theresienstadt from 21 April 1945 to 5 May 1945 at between 13,500 and 15,000 (*Theresienstadt*, 618). Lederer calculates that 9,000 prisoners arrived on 22 April 1945 and a few days later an additional 4,000 (*Ghetto Theresienstadt*, 186).

57.   Adler confirms these estimates: 7,000 prisoners from the Czech "Protectorate," 5,500 Germans, 1,250 Austrians, 1,250 Dutch, 1,400 Slovaks, 1,000 Hungarians (*Theresienstadt*, 618). These factions did not get along very well; there were often misinterpretations or tensions along political, national, religious, and linguistic lines. Redlich describes a toilet system in which German Jews were assigned to protect toilets (they locked from the outside), but they could not understand Czech numbers and so did not know when a Czech speaker was finished using the facilities and called out the number of his or her toilet stall (*The Terezin Diary*, 90).

58.   The United States Holocaust Memorial Museum estimates that in October 1944 there were 11,077 Jews in Theresienstadt ("Theresienstadt: Timeline," *Holocaust Encyclopedia*, www.ushmm.org/wlc/en/article.php ?ModuleId=10007460).

59.   Theresienstadt was policed by 28 SS men and between 150 and 170

Czech special unit gendarmerie soldiers (United States Holocaust Memorial Museum, "Theresienstadt: SS and Police Structure," *Holocaust Encyclopedia*, www.ushmm.org/wlc/en/article.php?ModuleId=10007462). On the policing of the camp see also Benz, *Theresienstadt*, 45–64.

60. On 5 May 1945 Rahm left Theresienstadt and fled into Austria. The United States arrested him in November 1945. In January 1947 he attempted to commit suicide but failed. Rahm was executed on 20 April 1947 (Benz, *Theresienstadt*, 49).

61. The order for forced abortions of pregnant women went out on 7 July 1943 (Adler, *Theresienstadt*, 121).

62. There were 230 births and 350 forced abortions in Theresienstadt (Adler, *Theresienstadt*, 269).

63. See Adler, *Theresienstadt*, 73–75, for an account of the public executions in 1942 for smuggling letters. The hangman that Eva here mentions was sent to Auschwitz and became a kapo. He died as a victim of medical experiments (Adler, *Theresienstadt*, 759).

64. Karl Bergel (b. 1902 in Dortmund) was a hairdresser and notorious drunkard, known for breaking the ribs and skulls of camp inhabitants. Gonda Redlich recalled Bergel shooting a cat on 2 May 1943 and shouting, "This is how a camp supervisor shoots!" (*The Terezin Diary*, 116). Rudolf Heindl (also spelled Haindl) was known for arresting prisoners because they carried cigarettes. He left the camp on 2 or 3 May 1945 and was arrested two years later in Salzburg. He was executed in September 1948; see Lederer, *Ghetto Theresienstadt*, 76–79.

65. There are several accounts of Heindl's cruelties. In another instance, he broke the neck of a woman carrying a folding chair as she entered the sluice (Adler, *Theresienstadt*, 754).

66. The first Theresienstadt prisoners arrived in November 1941; by the end of the year there were more than 5,365 from Prague and 2,000 from Brünn (Adler, *Theresienstadt*, 33).

67. Noack-Mosse here references Jews who went underground in Berlin during the Nazi campaign to make the city "free of Jews" (*Judenfrei*). The Gestapo worked to locate and deport these "U-Boote." Between 1943 and 1944 they had halved the number of underground Jews from four to two thousand. In Berlin there were fifteen to seventeen hundred Jews hidden by twenty to thirty thousand Germans through the Second World War. See Beate Meyer, Hermann Simon, Chana Schütz, eds., *Jews in Nazi Berlin: From Kristallnacht to Liberation* (Chicago: University of Chicago Press, 2009), 249.

68. Noack-Mosse's affection for her hometown is apparent throughout the diary. She draws a sharp distinction between the city she knew growing up and Nazi Berlin.

69. Noack-Mosse here criticizes the superficial improvements of the camp that were designed to impress international inspectors. The report prepared by Paul Dunant of the International Red Cross after visiting the camp in April 1945 suggests that the deception worked. Dunant did not believe the camp had been "specially prepared for outside guests" (Adler, *Theresienstadt*, 168–69).

70. For video testimony of this Red Cross visit see the documentary *Terezín Diary*, directed by Dan Weissman (New York: Jewish Media Fund, 1991), VHS. See also Lederer, *Ghetto Theresienstadt*, 100–101; Benz, *Theresienstadt*, 186–92; and United States Holocaust Memorial Museum, "Theresienstadt: Red Cross Visit," *Holocaust Encyclopedia*, www.ushmm.org/wlc/en/article .php?ModuleId=10007463.

71. The producer of the film was Karel Pečený (1899–1965) (Karel Margry, "Newsreels in Nazi-Occupied Czechoslovakia: Karel Peceny and His Newsreel Company Aktualita," *Historical Journal of Film, Radio and Television* 24, no. 1 [2004]: 69–117). The director, Kurt Gerron, was deported to Auschwitz after filming and murdered. The following day the gas chambers at Auschwitz were closed. The film was never completed and exists in fragmentary form.

72. For Eppstein, see note 23.

73. On the long process of preserving Theresienstadt as a site of Holocaust memory, see Benz's final chapter, "Theresienstadt heute" (*Theresienstadt*, 233–46).

74. There were roughly fifty people unaccounted for total. Adler argues that Seidl allowed Jakob Edelstein (1903–1944), the first Jewish Elder of Theresienstadt, to exempt more individuals from being deported East than the quotas called for and that this accounted for the discrepancy. See Adler, *Theresienstadt*, 129–33.

75. Those who experienced the 11 November 1943 count remembered it as a day of terror and agony. Gonda Redlich recalled, "They went and were counted. As if we were cattle or sheep. Darkness came, and the Jews planned to spend the night in the open field. Thirty-six thousand people, as docile as little children or sheep—lambs, standing and waiting" (*The Terezin Diary*, 135).

76. On 1 October 1941 a decree was issued forbidding Jews in the Protectorate of Bohemia and Moravia from smoking. Because Theresienstadt was in this zone of Nazi occupation, inmates in the camp were not allowed to smoke (Adler, *Theresienstadt*, 9).

77. This was approximately $2 in 1945, worth roughly $26 in 2017 (Robin Leonard Bidwell, *Currency Conversion Tables: A Hundred Years of Change* [London: Rex Collings, 1970], 23; Samuel H. Williamson, "Seven Ways to Compute the Relative Value of a U.S. Dollar Amount, 1774 to Present," *MeasuringWorth*, www.measuringworth.com/calculators/uscompare/index.php).

78. Adler, *Theresienstadt*, 25. The artist Norbert Troller (1896–1984) was also sent to the Small Fortress. See his description of his experience in his memoir *Theresienstadt: Hitler's Gift to the Jews,* ed. Joel Shatzky, trans. Susan E. Cernyak-Spatz (Chapel Hill: University of North Carolina Press, 1991), 141–60.

79. As Adler notes, those sent to the Small Fortress were "generally . . . not seen again." He calculates that a total of 239 individuals were sent to this fate between 1941 and 1944 (*Theresienstadt*, 40).

80. Parcels sent to the camp did not take much longer to arrive than normal post during the war. They were opened and inspected before being resealed and passed on to the camp Jewish postal service. During the inspection, the most prized items often went missing. In order to get packages to camp inmates, relatives had to follow a specific address format or risk outright confiscation: "Mr. X, Theresienstadt, Street No., Bauschowitz [Bohušovice] Post Office" (Adler, *Theresienstadt*, 510–11).

81. Germany occupied Denmark on 9 April 1940. German officials largely ignored the "Jewish question" in Denmark until September 1943. SS general Werner Best (1903–1989) warned German naval attaché Ferdinand Duckwitz (1904–1973) of the impending arrest of Danish Jews, and Duckwitz in turn warned Danish civilians. German authorities ultimately arrested 470 of the 7,500 Jews in Denmark and deported them to Theresienstadt, where 120 of them perished (United States Holocaust Memorial Museum, "Denmark," *Holocaust Encyclopedia*, www.ushmm.org/wlc/en/article.php?ModuleId =10005209).

82. See Bernd Wöbke, "Meyer, Richard Joseph, Chemiker," in *Neue Deutsche Biographie*, vol. 17 (Berlin: Duncker und Humblot, 1994), 369.

83. Joseph Goebbels (1897–1945) was Reich minister of propaganda during the Third Reich. His ministry portrayed Jews as racial enemies of Germans and dealt in stereotypes of what "Germans" and "Jews" looked like.

84. Adler calculates that by 1943 40 percent of Theresienstadt's prisoners were over 30 percent underweight. The most radical weight loss for inmates occurred during their first six months in the camp (*Theresienstadt*, 461).

85. In addition, the inmates tended rabbits, chickens, silk worms, and large farm animals (Adler, *Theresienstadt*, 194).

86. On the recovery of the Danish community from Theresienstadt, see also Caroline Moorehead, *Dunant's Dream: War, Switzerland and the History of the Red Cross* (London: HarperCollins, 1998), 465–66.

87. Moorehead, *Dunant's Dream*, 457–60.

88. On the transportation of the Danish Jews from Theresienstadt to Sweden, see Adler, *Theresienstadt*, 713–14.

89. Saul S. Friedman cites the release of Danish Jews and the burning of Theresienstadt records as part of Adolf Eichmann's (1906–1962) and Sicherheits-dienst chief Ernst Kaltenbrunner's (1903–1946) attempts to protect themselves after the war; see Redlich, *The Terezin Diary*, 162.

90. Johannes Holm (b. 1902) lived until at least 1984, when he published his memoir, *Sandheden om de hvide busser* (Copenhagen: Samleren, 1984). On the expedition, see Hans Sode-Madsen, "The Perfect Deception: The Danish Jews and Theresienstadt 1940–1945," *Leo Baeck Institute Year Book* 38 (1993): 263–90.

91. Oberscharführer Siegfried Seidl ordered the first executions in Theresien-stadt. Seidl kept dogs and was diligent about his uniform. On his desk he kept a caricature of a Jew with a caption that read "Don't get cross, always try to smile" (Lederer, *Ghetto Theresienstadt*, 74–75). Redlich reports that people in the camp believed Seidl hated Jews because when he was fourteen years old a Jew cheated his parents of their wealth. "This Jew came here. The camp com-mandant [Seidl] struck him and punished him with imprisonment. As a per-sonal revenge, this Jew was deprived of food every other day. An old man" (*The Terezin Diary*, 104).

92. Dunant visited the camp on 6 April 1945, escorted by Adolf Eichmann (Adler, *Theresienstadt*, 164; Hannah Arendt, *Eichmann in Jerusalem: A Report on the Banality of Evil* [New York: Viking, 1964], 146).

93. Adler, *Theresienstadt*, 173–75. Dunant returned to Theresienstadt on 2 May. The SS continued to kill prisoners in the Small Fortress, but by 3 May its remaining inmates had been moved into barracks. Rahm left the camp on the morning of 6 May 1945.

94. Benito Mussolini (1883–1945) was executed on 28 April 1945. The news of his death reached Theresienstadt two days later.

95. Adolf Hitler (1889–1945) committed suicide in Berlin on 30 April 1945.

96. Dr. Leo Baeck arrived in Theresienstadt in 1943 (Adler, *Theresienstadt*, 127). Alfred Meissner (1871–1950). Klang's first name was actually Heinrich (1875–1954). Eduard's last name was actually Meijers (1880–1954). Before the Germans left Theresienstadt, leaders in the camp secretly met and selected Jiří Vogel to take over camp administration. The Jewish Council of Elders dissolved

once Vogel stepped in as mayor of the camp on 5 May 1945 (Lederer, *Ghetto Theresienstadt*, 191).

97. The battle outside of Theresienstadt took place 6–7 May 1945 (Adler, *Theresienstadt*, 618).

98. The grenade was thrown by a Russian soldier; an Austrian colonel was killed and a Dutch general died a few days later from his wounds (Adler, *Theresienstadt*, 175).

99. The Russians worked quickly after formally entering the camp on 9 May. They established five hospitals and a delousing station. They isolated everyone thought to have typhus and disinfected them. There were approximately thirty thousand prisoners in the camp when the Red Army arrived (Lederer, *Ghetto Theresienstadt*, 194–95; United States Holocaust Memorial Museum, "Theresienstadt: Timeline," www.ushmm.org/wlc/en/article.php?ModuleId =10007460).

100. Benz, *Theresienstadt*, 203; Adler, *Theresienstadt*, 176.

101. The Red Army instituted strict quarantine procedures on 14 May to contain the typhus epidemic (Adler, *Theresienstadt*, 619). From 6 to 19 May roughly 2,950 camp occupants contracted the disease, of which 502 died, amounting to a 22.9 percent mortality rate (Lederer, *Ghetto Theresienstadt*, 195).

102. David Graham (1912–1999) covered the liberation of Theresienstadt for the BBC. On the BBC and the Final Solution see Gabriel Milland, "Some Faint Hope and Courage: The BBC and the Final Solution, 1942–1945" (PhD diss., University of Leicester, 1998).

103. Adler also notes Klaus Mann's visit; see *Theresienstadt*, 685.

104. The "four well-known knocks" Noack-Mosse here describes were the opening four notes of Beethoven's Fifth Symphony. This was part of a larger BBC campaign to use Beethoven's famous score as Morse code for "V" (dot-dot-dot-dash) or "victory." The campaign appropriated a German composer to indicate the eventual German defeat. Matthew Guerrieri, *The First Four Notes: Beethoven's Fifth and the Human Imagination* (New York: Alfred A. Knopf, 2012), 211–15. See also the Allied propaganda poster at www.cmuse.org /beethovens-fifth-symphony-and-morse-code/.

105. See "Vedder, Aron 1904–1964," Database Joods Biografisch Woordenboek: Joden in Nederland in de twintigste eeuw, www.jodeninnederland.nl/id /P-3347.

106. Eva Noack-Mosse here drew on Adler's study of Theresienstadt to corroborate her statistical information.

107. On Martha Mosse after the war, see Kraus, *Die Familie Mosse*, 590–91.

108. Hans (1918–1943) and Sophie (1921–1943) Scholl were siblings who

helped found and organize the "White Rose" resistance against National Socialism. They published and distributed leaflets calling for passive resistance against the Nazi regime around the Ludwig-Maximilians-Universität in Munich. Both were arrested and executed in 1943. On the Scholls, see Inge Scholl, *The White Rose: Munich, 1942–1943* (Middletown, CT: Wesleyan University Press, 1983).

109. Carl Zuckmayer also wrote the screenplay for *Der blaue Engel*, based on Heinrich Mann's novel *Professor Unrat*. See also his autobiography, *Als wär's ein Stück von mir: Horen der Freundschaft* (Frankfurt: Fischer, 1966).

Appendix 1: Correspondence between Eva Noack-Mosse and George L. Mosse

1. Noack-Mosse here references a highly controversial 1951 novel by Ernst von Salomon; see his entry in the glossary.

2. Noack-Mosse is likely discussing a speech General Douglas MacArthur (1880–1964) gave the previous year to Congress, in April 1951. In this speech MacArthur quoted one of the songs he sang while in basic training: "Old Soldiers Never Die; They Just Fade Away."

3. In 1952, when this letter was composed, Adlai Stevenson II (1900–1965) was the governor of Illinois and campaigning for the presidency of the United States, a bid he would lose to General Dwight D. Eisenhower (1890–1969).

4. The (anonymous) article to which Eva is referring here is "Triumph for Terrorism," *Time*, 15 October 1973, 40–47. This article dealt with the Austrian government's response to a hostage-taking attack by Palestinian terrorists in the town of Marchegg. Bruno Kreisky (1911–1990), a man of Jewish origin, was chancellor of Austria at the time. According to the *Time* article, "experts like University of Wisconsin Historian George L. Mosse, who contend that Austria remains 'unreconstructedly anti-Semitic,' wonder if Kreisky acceded to the terrorists' demands partly to prove how genuinely Austrian he is."

Appendix 2: Glossary of Names

1. Philipp Manes, *As If It Were Life: A WWII Diary from the Theresienstadt Ghetto* (New York: Palgrave Macmillan, 2009), 91.

2. See Zdenek Lederer, *Ghetto Theresienstadt* (New York: Howard Fertig, 1983), 76–78.

3. See George E. Berkley, *Hitler's Gift: The Story of Theresienstadt* (Boston: Branden Books, 1993), 81–82.

4. Elsa Bernstein, *Das Leben als Drama: Erinnerungen an Theresienstadt*, ed. Rita Bake and Birgit Kiupel (Hamburg: Landeszentrale für politische Bildung, 2005), 173.

5. See Thomas Corinth, *Lovis Corinth: Eine Dokumentation* (Tübingen: Ernst Wasmuth, 1979).

6. Yves Laplace, *Plaine des héros* (Paris: Fayard, 2015), 261, 269–70, 277.

7. H. G. Adler, *Theresienstadt, 1941–1945: The Face of a Coerced Community*, ed. Amy Loewenhaar-Blauweiss, trans. Belinda Cooper (Cambridge: Cambridge University Press, 2017), 164, 175.

8. For an image, see Library of Congress Prints and Photographs Division, Washington, DC, LC-USZ62-137859, www.loc.gov/pictures/item /2008676241. For a sympathetic biography, see Helen Sheehy, *Eleonora Duse: A Biography* (New York: Knopf, 2003).

9. Marita Krauss, ed., *Rechte Karrieren in München: Von der Weimarer Zeit bis in die Nachkriegsjahre* (Munich: Volk, 2010), 220–24.

10. See John Mendelsohn, comp., *Nuernberg War Crimes Trials: Records of Case IX, United States of America v. Otto Ohlendorf et al.* (Washington, DC: National Archives and Records Service, General Services Administration, 1978), 76.

11. Andreas Grote, ed., *Verlagsort Berlin: 100 Jahre Ullstein; Eine Ausstellung der Staatlichen Museen Preussischer Kulturbesitz und des Axel Springer Verlages, Sonderausstellungshalle, Berlin-Dahlem 15. Juni–31. Juli 1977* (Berlin: Ullstein/ Axel Springer, 1977).

12. "Das Institut für Museumsforschung der Staatlichen Museen zu Berlin trauert um seinen Gründungsdirektor Dr. Andreas Grote," Institut für Museumsforschung, 28 January 2015, www.smb.museum/nachrichten/detail/das -institut-fuer-museumsforschung-der-staatlichen-museen-zu-berlin-trauert -um-seinen-gruendungsdirekt.html.

13. For a brief autobiographical sketch, see Alfred von Klement, *Die Bücher von Otto Erich Hartleben: Eine Bibliographie mit der bisher unveröffentlichten ersten Fassung der Selbstbiographie des Dichters und hundert Abbildungen* (Salò: Halkyonische Akademie für unangewandte Wissenschaften, 1951).

14. "Haindl Rudolf," Yad Vashem, http://db.yadvashem.org/deportation /supervisorsDetails.html?language=en&itemId=7451560.

15. Elisabeth Kraus, *Die Familie Mosse: Deutsch-jüdisches Bürgertum im 19. und 20. Jahrhundert* (Munich: Beck, 1999), 299.

16. Lederer, *Ghetto Theresienstadt*, 174.

17. This book was republished in 2016 by Princeton University Press.

18. For an overview of Laband's career, see Manfred Friedrich, "Laband, Paul," in *Neue Deutsche Biographie*, vol. 13 (Berlin: Duncker und Humblot, 1982), 362–63.

19. *Gedenkbuch Berlins: Der jüdischen Opfer des Nationalsozialismus* (Berlin: Hentrich, 1995), 752, 756.

20. For an overview of Heinrich Mann's biography, see Klaus Schröter, "Mann, Heinrich," in *Neue Deutsche Biographie*, vol. 16 (Berlin: Duncker und Humblot, 1990), 39–43.

21. For an overview of Klaus Mann's biography, see Hiltrud Häntzschel, "Mann, Klaus," in *Neue Deutsche Biographie*, vol. 16, 51–54.

22. For an overview of Thomas Mann's biography, see Klaus Schröter, "Mann, Thomas," in *Neue Deutsche Biographie*, vol. 16, 43–50.

23. See Alex Rössle, "Jagdflieger und Zeichner Hannes Otto Trautloft (1912–1995)," *Oberstdorf-Lexikon*, www.oberstdorf-lexikon.de/trautloft-hannes -otto.html.

24. George L. Mosse, *Confronting History: A Memoir* (Madison: University of Wisconsin Press, 2000), 73.

25. For a recent discussion of Martha Mosse's biography see Javier Semper Vendrell, "The Case of a German-Jewish Lesbian Woman: Martha Mosse and the Danger of Standing Out," *German Studies Review* 41, no. 2 (May 2018): 335–53.

26. Kraus, *Die Familie Mosse*, 307–8.

27. Adler, *Theresienstadt*, 243.

28. "Rahm, Karl," Ghetto-Theresienstadt: Theresienstadt 1941–1945—Ein Nachschlagewerk, www.ghetto-theresienstadt.info/pages/r/rahmk.htm.

29. See *Gedenkbuch Berlins*, 1127.

30. Ralf Hoffrogge, *A Jewish Communist in Weimar Germany: The Life of Werner Scholem (1895–1940)*, trans. Loren Balhorn and Jan-Peter Herrmann (Boston: Brill, 2017), 585. See also Scholem's account of this tragedy in Marion Kaplan, *Between Dignity and Despair: Jewish Life in Nazi Germany* (New York: Oxford University Press, 1998), 93.

31. Shaul Magid, "Gershom Scholem," *Stanford Encyclopedia of Philosophy*, ed. Edward N. Zalta, https://plato.stanford.edu/archives/sum2014/entries /scholem.

32. See Jürgen Matthäus, *Jewish Responses to Persecution, 1941–1942* (Lanham, MD: AltaMira Press, 2013), 299–300.

33. Their exchange is available in translation as part of Yale Law School's Avalon Project; see http://avalon.law.yale.edu/imt/03-14-46.asp.

34. See Gudrun Maierhof, *Selbstbehauptung im Chaos: Frauen in der jüdischen Selbsthilfe 1933–1943* (Frankfurt: Campus Verlag, 2001), 272.

35. See Robert S. Wistrich, *Who's Who in Nazi Germany* (New York: Macmillan, 1982), 217.

36. For a picture of Amalie with her husband, Carl, see Gunther Nickel, ed., *Carl Zuckmayer, Albrecht Joseph: Briefwechsel 1922–1972* (Göttingen: Wallstein, 2007), 452. See also Gunther Nickel and Ulrike Weiß, eds., *Carl Zuckmayer 1896–1977: "Ich wollte nur Theater machen"* (Marbach am Neckar: Deutsche Schillergesellschaft, 1996), 19.

37. See also Zuckmayer's published correspondence in Nickel, *Carl Zuckmayer, Albrecht Joseph.*

Index

cheese. *See under* food
children, 69–71, 77, 156n30, 158nn48–49, 159n52
The Children of the King (Rosmer), 61, 139
chocolate. *See under* food
cigarettes, 82, 86, 104, 109–10, 161n76
city of the Jews, 26. *See also* Theresienstadt
clothing, 18, 30, 39, 45, 51
coffee, 33, 43, 92
Cohn, Emil (great-uncle), 141–42
Cohn, Leonore (great-aunt), 131, 142
concentration camps. *See* camps
The Constitutional Law of the German Reich (Laband), 143
contraband, 50
Corinth, Lovis, 36, 140
Cossmann, Oskar, 140
Council of the Elders, 50, 106, 139–40, 163n96
crime, 11, 37, 70, 74, 82–83
Czech-German tension, xxii
Czechoslovakia, xix, 97–98

Danish government, 83–84
Danziger, Alfred (brother-in-law), xix, 140, 145
Danziger, Hilde (sister), xix, 114, 140, 145
Das Leben als Drama: Erinnerungen an Theresienstadt (Bernstein), 139
Das Staatsrecht des Deutschen Reiches (Laband), 143
David Copperfield (Dickens), 59, 144
death camps. *See* camps
deaths: of Hitler, 104; of prisoners sent to camps from Theresienstadt, xxi, xxii, 67–68, 153n12, 155n26; rates of, 139, 151n11; and remains, 79; at Theresienstadt, xxi, 67–68, 71, 74, 84, 102–3, 115–19, 159n52
dentists, 19, 54
Der blaue Engel, 143, 148
dermatologists, 54

Der Zauberberg (Mann), 144
diarrhea, 33
"Diary of a Survivor" (Noack-Mosse), xxiv
Die Tat, 134
Die Welt, 131
disease, 33, 58, 69, 89, 102–3, 158n44. *See also* epidemics; quarantine; typhoid; typhus
disinfection, 30, 33
doctors, 54, 89, 100, 102, 119, 155n25
Duckwitz, Ferdinand, 162n81
Dunant, Paul, 101, 105–6, 109, 140, 161n69, 163n93
Duse, Eleonora, 140
Dutch-Indian Council, 59

eczema, 43
Ehrhardt, Hermann, 128
Eichendorff, Joseph von, 47
Eichmann, Adolf, 140
Eisenhower, Dwight, 165n3
Entwesung, 30
epidemics, xxii, 68, 71, 100, 119, 158n44. *See also* disease; quarantine; typhoid; typhus
Eppstein, Paul, 78, 140
eye clinic, 54–55

farmland, 120
fat. *See under* food
Ferdinand, Franz, 82
flashlights, 27, 44
fleas, 43
Fontane, Theodor, 65
food: bread, 27, 33, 43–45, 64–65, 68, 76, 82, 112, 120; butter, 27, 69, 125; cheese, 79–80, 84, 86, 125; chocolate, 96, 107, 110, 158n46; coupons, 18–19, 151n16; distribution point, 33, 43–44, 51, 64, 66; fat, 43, 77, 112; gravy, 33; meat, 33, 51, 68, 80, 86, 112; potatoes, 33, 37, 51, 65–66, 68, 75, 86, 99, 112,

George L. Mosse Series in
Modern European Cultural and Intellectual History

Series Editors

**Steven E. Aschheim, Skye Doney, Mary Louise Roberts, and
David J. Sorkin**

Of God and Gods: Egypt, Israel, and the Rise of Monotheism
Jan Assmann

The Enemy of the New Man: Homosexuality in Fascist Italy
Lorenzo Benadusi;
translated by Suzanne Dingee and Jennifer Pudney

*The Holocaust and the West German Historians: Historical Interpretation and
Autobiographical Memory*
Nicolas Berg;
translated and edited by Joel Golb

Collected Memories: Holocaust History and Postwar Testimony
Christopher R. Browning

Cataclysms: A History of the Twentieth Century from Europe's Edge
Dan Diner;
translated by William Templer with Joel Golb

La Grande Italia: The Myth of the Nation in the Twentieth Century
Emilio Gentile;
translated by Suzanne Dingee and Jennifer Pudney

The Invisible Jewish Budapest: Metropolitan Culture at the Fin de Siècle
Mary Gluck

Jews and Other Germans: Civil Society, Religious Diversity, and Urban Politics in Breslau, 1860–1925
Till van Rahden;
translated by Marcus Brainard

An Uncompromising Generation: The Nazi Leadership of the Reich Security Main Office
Michael Wildt;
translated by Tom Lampert